Millennial Initiates

Millennial Initiates

Ben Ellis

Published by
CulturallyShifted, LLC.
2019

© 2019 Ben Ellis and CulturallyShifted, LLC. All rights reserved. The moral right of the author has been asserted.

No part of this publication may be reproduced, distributed, or transmitted in any form or by any means, including photocopying, recording, or other electronic or mechanical methods, without the prior written permission of the publisher, except in the case of brief quotations embodied in critical reviews and certain other noncommercial uses permitted by copyright law. For permission requests, write or email to the publisher, addressed "Attention: Permissions Coordinator," at the address below.

CulturallyShifted, LLC
P.O. Box 471425
District Heights, MD 20753
info@culturallyshifted.com
www.culturallyshifted.com

Printed in the United States of America
First Printing, 2019
ISBN 13: 978-1-7340451-0-9

DEDICATION

To my amazing wife, I love you! Thank you, without your love, support and inspiration I could have never accomplished this dream of mine. To our dear daughter, always know that there is no ceiling! With thoughts, ideas and organized planning there is nothing you cannot accomplish.

Contents

Acknowledgements
Preface
Introduction

I. Shining Light On Spiritual Warfare……..pg. 03

II. Know Thyself……………………….pg. 10

III. The Story of Ausar……………………pg. 15

IV. The Eye of Heru and The Pineal Gland….pg. 20

V. 7 Hermetic Principles of Tehuti………….pg. 26

VI. Removing The Wool…………………….pg. 34

VII. Mindfulness Meditation………………….pg. 44

VIII. Eat To Live……………………………pg. 57

IX. To Conquer A Demon! (Shaking alcoholism).pg. 68

X. Manifest Abundance!……………………pg. 79

XI. The Spirit of Love…………………….pg. 88

About the Author
Glossary of Terms
11 Kemetic Axioms
11 Conscious Resources

Acknowledgements

I would like to thank my teachers, professors, and my family without whose help this book would never have been completed. Thank you for always supporting my vision and encouraging me to pursue my dreams with unyielding force!

Thank you to all of my mentors, coaches and colleagues who in some way, shape or form contributed to the person I am today. To all who view this publication, I love you. We are all one, just in a varying incarnation. Never be afraid to become the light that you seek!

Preface

Growing up, certain ideals and beliefs were set into my psyche from both family and society. Things like go to school, get a good job, be a good "Christian" and a die-hard Washington sports fanatic. Even finite things such as my appearance were shaped by the influence of society. One day that all changed.

My wife and I would often have very deep discussions about life and why we as a collective tend to accept certain "norms" as law. In questioning societal norms and researching the origins of many so called truths, we began to notice we'd been living in a figurative Twilight Zone. Newly married, with a child on the way, we had to unlearn almost everything we'd been taught growing up in order to create our own family dynamic independent from expectations.

A few weeks after our daughter was born we decided to embrace a plant based lifestyle free of all meat and dairy. This because we wanted to ensure that we were doing everything in our power to be healthy, here for her, setting good habits and an example for her to see how to live a healthy life.

In a domino like fashion, following the plant-based lifestyle adjustment came mindfulness meditation, then quitting alcohol and starting a business. The man that I had been up until age 30 was no more. Life in each moment became the most beautiful thing to experience and with a clear vision I knew I could accomplish anything I set my mind to. But as I observed the landscape of my fellow human, particularly those in my generation and below, I understood what I needed to do.

I wrote this book in effort to give what I have learned and experienced, to all who it can have a positive effect upon. Millennial Initiates is not a dogmatic, authoritarian guideline to tell folks how to live their lives. It is rather, a grouping of ideals both spiritual and practical that can aid the reader in finding their own light within. Centuries of misinformation has led us to this place in time where individuals are living a life controlled by emotion and impulse. This text will expose some of that misinformation and use ancient African spirituality in conjunction with present day science to guide the reader to a more mindful way of living. I entitled this work Millennial Initiates to represent the present day awakening of a generation not indifferent from the ancient Egyptian initiations of old.

I drew inspiration from works such as "The Metu-Neter" by Dr. Ra Un Nefer Amen, "The Kybalion" by three initiates and "The Emerald Tablets of Thoth" translated by Dr. Michael Doreal just to name a few. These esoteric, philosophical works combined with the aforementioned dialogues between my wife and I, filled my mind with a vast amount of information that needed to be shared. I hope within the text of this book you find principles that may add value to your life.

Through the space and time that separate us I extend my hand in friendship as the light in me greets the light within you. Namaste.

Author
Ben Ellis

Introduction

The odds of us being born are 400 Trillion to one! We are not accidents; we are here in divine order. The seemingly endless chain link of events in a cycle of cause and effect leading up to birth is simply unfathomable! Nonetheless, here we are. The unseen miracle lies within the atom of every cell that is us. Yet, due to unfortunate events over the last few hundred years, which are a blink in the infinity of time, the culture of our beloved black community finds itself searching for a new identity. We've witnessed the first African American President, some have seen higher economic prosperity, and we are more educated than ever! But still there seems to be a disconnect as many of us are attempting to rediscover our ancestral roots pre-slavery. There is a collective spark that lies dormant within us as a collective. It has been forgotten and in many of us it has yet to even come into knowledge of its own existence. Buried beneath a seemingly immovable weight of ego and false self-identification, yet not extinguished. It lies dormant awaiting the chance that it might come to know itself and bring forth unprecedented power not before seen in its own image. That hibernation is over!

Peel back the veil of the Maya! Mindless entertainment, deceit filled history books, poison on plates and served on the rocks. ENOUGH!

Embedded within these words shines the LIGHT of a new day! An unyielding force as bright as the morning sunrise, fanning the spark within all who absorb its message, that it might illuminate into a blaze giving rise unto the next golden age of mankind! The information age has brought with it a revived consciousness not seen since the time of the ancients. Combined with the mitochondrial DNA and cellular memory passed down through the ages, we are witness to the revived spirit of the ancestors!

GRAND RISING MILLENNIAL INITIATES!

So let it be.

I. Shining Light on Spiritual Warfare

True teaching is not an accumulation of knowledge; it is an awakening of consciousness.
~Kemetic Axiom

There is a war taking place in the world of the unseen. There are no guns, rockets or explosive devices, but don't be fooled, the weapon of choice is more destructive to an individual than an atomic bomb. This war is the battlefield of the mind! In order to illuminate that which is hidden, to shine light on matters of spiritual warfare, let us first gain a greater inner, under and "over-standing" as to what exactly is "spirit". This is of great significance before we can address any further topic as we will see that spirit is the essence of all. In ancient times our ancestors throughout the globe used the term "spirit" to describe the unseen forces that shape all matter in existence. Natural phenomena and elements such as the sun, the moon, fire, water, air and earth were regarded as deity and given humanlike characteristics. There were even spirit representations to the properties of our own consciousness, which we will most especially analyze throughout this work.

Now as it relates to human beings, what we must realize is that what our ancestors referred to as spirit, science today describes as "subconscious". You see modern science uses this phrase in its efforts to describe the unseen force within each of us. While the word spirit prompts skepticism when trying to define matters of great mystery, the term "subconscious" is a much safer approach for scientific study. Going forward I may tend to use both depending on the context, but do not make the mistake of identifying the words as having a separate fundamental meaning.

I want you to do something. Close your eyes, take a deep breath and say to yourself "I am amazing!" Take a moment now to do so. You didn't say this out loud, you said it to yourself. So let me ask you this; whose voice was that? Where did it come from? Was it your subconscious? Maybe, perhaps. Now let's try something different. If you would just close your eyes again, take another deep breath, and this time just feel your heart beating and feel the tingling in your extremities. Now ask yourself this, "what is it that is controlling these masterful designs inside of me?" Science says that it is the faculties of your subconscious mind which regulates over 95% of your daily actions.

The ancestors refer to it as spirit, the life force within that holds many titles across all cultures. In ancient Kemet, what we now refer to as Egypt (a Greek name) it is referred to as the "Ra", in Chinese Taoism it is known as the "Chi", the force that sustains the universe.

In just the last two hundred years science has come to recognize that the atom is the building block to all matter including our cells. Perhaps most important to this discovery is the fact that atoms are composed of a concentration of energy. So then one might ask, "well what is energy?" Energy is defined as "a fundamental entity of nature that is transferred between parts of a system in the production of physical change within the system and usually regarded as the capacity for doing work" (Merriam-Webster's Dictionary, 2016). If we remember what the term spirit was used to describe by the ancients, and energy as it relates to nature, we see that the two are in fact synonymous.

All is energy. There are no lines of separation when we recognize this. Every physical material, organism and substance in existence are all composed of atoms, thus vibrations of energy. Living in this realization is what's referred to as being aligned with one's higher self. At our core, the building block of our make-up is purely vibrations of energy. The illusion of separation is what has led to mankind's downfall. This idea that you and I are separate when in fact we are one, just a varying incarnation of the source energy flowing through us. Through greater understanding of what we are as a collective, we as a species can begin to make decisions and take actions that are best for all living beings and the progress of the planet.

So, when speaking on matters of spiritual warfare, what we are actually dealing with is the battle for our energy that takes place both internally and externally. Within our own consciousness we're faced with a battlefield of choices between good and evil on an everyday basis. Outside of us, there are countless entities that seek to influence our thinking and steer our actions. Spiritual warfare is very real, but without knowledge of self it often goes undetected.

The blueprint to victory in the internal battle rests in our belief systems. Our perception shapes our perspective, which then molds our beliefs and thoughts. Do you see the chain link here? The thoughts then resonate in our words and actions so ask yourself, do I have a limiting belief? All is mental and to break any generational curse we must first get rid of a negative belief. Here are 8 steps to do so:

1. The first thing that we have to do is recognize that it's all BS! Belief Systems. When someone doubts you or you doubt yourself, that's BS!

2. Question the thoughts that come into your mind. Once you change your mind you change your reality! We have to change that programming. Many of us don't recognize that our beliefs simply aren't true. We have to stop a limiting belief before it grows! For example, I used to think that I could not be an entrepreneur, I can't quit my 9-5 and work for myself. That's a limiting belief. I changed those thoughts to "How can I become an entrepreneur"? By transforming our belief our body and mind will

no longer be limited to a box. Then by turning the statement "I can't", into a question "How can I", we open up our mind to the possibilities and begin to conceive a way!

3. Change your habits! Are you stuck on a conveyer belt lifestyle? Wake up, go to work, come home and eat. Repeat. Get away from what the crowd is doing! Start rewriting your story line. Everyday wake up knowing you are living in infinite abundance! Start with subtle changes. Wake up earlier to give yourself 30 minutes to set your intention for the day. Use your lunch break to work toward ways to break the cycle. When you come home, rather than engaging in mindless entertainment, start researching and taking action towards your dreams!

4. Find an example! Look for proof that your dream is possible. You don't have to re-invent the wheel. Lots of times there is someone or even multiple people who have already accomplished what you are trying to do. Use their example and make it your own.

5. Believe that the world is working in your favor! If you think the whole world is against you, that's what you will attract. The universe gives us what we are believing. If you are on the highway looking for number synchronicity I

promise you will notice every 444 or 222 on the license plates of cars you pass by.

6. Reprogram your subconscious mind! Now we're getting into the depths of things. Our subconscious mind governs over 95% of our life. The language of the subconscious mind is imagery. So if we use more empowering imagery we are priming our subconscious mind. If you want abundance try hanging up a large print out of that house you want. Your subconscious mind will begin to work towards that goal even when you aren't consciously aware of it. It's like driving a car to a familiar destination. You look up and you've arrived but you can't even remember what happened along the way because your subconscious mind took over.

7. Ask yourself, is this belief serving me? If you are thinking thoughts like "I'm not good enough for that promotion"? Let go of that belief! Let go of any belief that doesn't empower you. It's pointless thinking about something that makes you feel bad. The more we let go of those thoughts, the more the scale tips to making us feel empowered!

8. There is belief, and there is knowing! Many of us believe because we don't know! Navigate into the realm of knowing by producing organized plans and taking measurable steps!

Once you've done it, you don't have to believe you can do it, you know you can do it because you've done it before! Then keep on "doing it, and doing it, and doing it well!" Like LL Cool J.

When I first thought about going vegan and quitting alcohol, my first thoughts were "oh, that's not going to happen, maybe for a few weeks, at most a month", but I certainly didn't think I could transform into an individual living a sober plant based lifestyle. Once I took action and started to feel the change in my body, I wanted to keep going. Before I knew it, 6 months had passed by, then a year, and next thing I knew I no longer held any desire for meat, dairy or alcohol. My subconscious mind had been reprogrammed, so much so that I don't even react to the smell of meat on the grill. The same goes with starting a business. I've never took any leap into entrepreneurship before in my life, but once my wife and I jumped in headfirst, things began to align. I began to watch more documentaries on entrepreneurship and read about successful entrepreneurs who started their business while still working a full time job. It gave me inspiration to know that I'm not the first, certainly not the last, to jump headfirst into following my dreams!

Don't let your own thoughts or the beliefs of others get in your way. Take action, move from believing into knowing! That's how you change your beliefs, and come out victorious on the internal battlefield of the larger Spiritual war.

II. Know Thyself

Know the world in yourself. Never look for yourself in the world, this would be to project your illusion. ~ Kemetic Axiom

In ancient Kemet, the phrase "Know Thyself" was engraved atop the entrance to every temple. The phrase served as a reminder for all who entered to identify with their higher self and to leave the ego, emotions, sensations and cravings at the door. These temples became referred to as "Mystery Schools" due to the advanced knowledge and wisdom imparted therein. A system of education centered on the spiritual cultivation of its students (referred to as "initiates"), extracting the internal as opposed to implanting the external.

Before one could begin down this path of learning, they would first undergo a period of fasting and meditation in order to cleanse the mind and body, readying themselves for this spiritual and psychological undertaking. What the ancients knew was that our existence is much more than the physical shell we occupy, and through a sequence of initiations the students would find their Light within. Coming forth in this awakening day by day, the initiate recognizes that within him or herself there is an automation regulating the heartbeat, metabolism, hormones and all of the subconscious faculties. An involuntary function that is one with all of nature, the universe above, the atoms below, and the source of all creation.

"What if the willed part of our being, instead of learning from the nescient will of others, learned from the omniscient being that directs the automation within us?" (Dr. Ra Un Nefer Amen, The Metu Neter volume 1: The Great Oracle of Tehuti and The Egyptian System of Spiritual Cultivation, 1990) This is precisely what the ancients were able to do through an array of rituals and meditations. Instructed unto the initiates so that they may tap into this omnipotence and come to "Know Thyself".

Science today continues to affirm these teachings. The late Dr. Carl Sagan, an American physicist, cosmologist and astrobiologist, notably stated that "We are a way for the cosmos to know itself" (Dr. Carl Sagan, Cosmos, 1980). A profound realization with strong basis, especially if we consider the fact that the human body is composed of the same elements found in the stars. Philosophers of many generations have posed questions grappling with the deeper meaning to life and our relationship with the cosmos. Some will find such questions to be futile as the finite mind of humans attempting to fully comprehend the mysteries of the universe could be considered akin to an atom in the stomach understanding the workings of the brain. But if we set aside skepticism and examine history, we come to find that fact is often more fascinating then fiction.

Take for instance the Dogon tribe of Mali, whom to this day still reside in West Africa and are the last known descendants of ancient Kemet. This civilization possessed knowledge of the stars Sirius A & B, one of which is invisible to the human eye, over 400 years before the telescope was invented! So is it that we are incapable of understanding the universe, or are we looking external when perhaps we should be searching within?

"A picture is worth a thousand words", this due to the mental influence of imagery in conveying thoughts. The people of Kemet held a great mastery of this principle and used it to create an advanced form of communication the world has yet to duplicate. "Metu-Neter", meaning "the words of nature", was the language of the ancients, referred to today as "Hieroglyphs" (a Greek name). The word "Neter", meaning nature, was also used to reference the deities. A great hidden truth is that the "Gods of Egypt" were actually personifications of natural phenomena in nature as well as our own consciousness. By personifying these divine occurrences, our ancestors had successfully created easy to understand metaphors used to instruct initiates on complex concepts in psychology, Earth science, Chemistry, Astrology and so on. Those involved in the discipline of psychology would quickly identify that the imagery used by the ancients speaks effectively to one's subconscious.

I attribute many of the troubles in the world today to a lost knowledge of self. True as it may be, we have to eliminate this victim mindset that somehow change must occur in the government or the economic power structure. The truth is that we are co-creators of our own existence and that we are the universe!

If we can recognize the truth that we are all one with nature and the source of creation, we can shift the global culture to a level not seen since the last golden age (26,000 years ago). It is my opinion that our ancestors building of the pyramids, aligned perfectly with Orion's belt, was not left here for us to simply marvel at and give praise. I estimate that they were erected for their symbolic nature and as a reminder to us that the forces governing the cosmos above so to exist in the atoms below. Metu-Neter was carved in stone so that no matter how far off course mankind strayed away, we can always remember to look within and KNOW THYSELF.

There is an old African story, in fact it is the oldest recorded story in history, that speaks to what it means to be in line with our higher selves and the consequences that derive when we are not. I'm going to summarize the ancient Kemetic story of Ausar which lives today through our expansion of consciousness! We will first visit the legend, then secondly examine its relationship to self.

III. The Story of Ausar

Know Thyself... and thou shalt know the gods.
~Kemetic Axiom

Ausar was a God-King, ruling over Kemet and loved by the people therein. He instructed his people on the ways of agriculture and irrigation, showed them how to build homes, and gave instruction to the use of writing with the hieroglyphic script (Invented by Tehuti, so much more to follow on him in chapter 5). Ausar's brother, Set, became jealous of Ausar and in his rage he then Killed him. To add insult, he dismembered Ausar's body into 14 pieces and spread it across the land. Auset, wife of Ausar, despite her grieving she would go on to then search for and collect the pieces of her husband's body. She then repositioned each limb, and wrapped the body in satin cloth, making Ausar the first mummy. Up until Ausar's death, he and Auset had no children. After he died, Auset is then impregnated by the spirit of Ausar and immaculately conceives their son, Heru, the rightful heir to Ausars throne. For his own protection, the Widows son is raised in secrecy near the wetlands of the Nile Delta. Once in adulthood, Heru goes to war with Set but is unable to defeat him through the course of many battles. In fact, Heru lost an eye during battle which would have to be healed by Tehuti. Despite being Uncertain of himself and feeling down and out from the defeat, Heru would receive some good wholesome instructions from an unlikely source. Ausar speaks to his son using Tehuti as essentially a mouthpiece. He provides the wisdom necessary for Heru to move forward and conquer his evil uncle. Armed with the Sword of Wisdom, Heru spares no time in defeating Set. Heru, Auset & Tehuti are then able to resurrect Ausar by giving his body the Eye of Heru. With the return of Ausar, order is re-established throughout the kingdom.

    I should note here that there are other versions of this story where Auset is unable to recover the penis of

Ausar. This is because it had been thrown into Nile River and swallowed by a fish. It is for this reason that fish would become forbidden to eat throughout the land (lots to cover on food and nutrition later).

Now that we've visited the legendary tale, let's analyze its hidden meaning. Ausar is representative of the God within and higher self, the oneness with all of creation and the source of creation. Set is a personification of our lower self. That animal spirit which is the ego, emotions, cravings & sensations that divide and separate us from our true higher self (this is why the head of Set is that of a Jackal. It is emblematic to one's animal nature). When our emotions get the best of us, it alludes to Set defeating Ausar and dividing him into 14 pieces. Think about how after an argument or dispute you later realize that you were acting out of character. In that moment you were identifying with the emotions felt rather than seeing things clearly. Auset collecting the body parts is representative to the beginning of our process to reconnect with our higher self. Heru is symbolic of our WILL power to overcome our emotions and lower self but we find that our will is not enough to conquer the impulses of our lower self, Set. That is until it is accompanied by wisdom which is symbolized as Tehuti. If nothing else, takeaway this understanding of using your own wisdom in conjunction with WILL power to overcome any obstacle in life! What separates us as humans from animals is our free will. Animals live in a state of enslavement to their impulses whereas we homo-sapiens have the ability to choose whether or not we will act out of emotion. The resurrection of Ausar illustrates our becoming into our own divinity, and re-establishing order within our temple (mind, body & spirit).

If you were brought up in a Christian household, as was I, certain aspects of this story may seem all but too familiar, and it should. Ausar, Auset & Heru represent the original sacred trinity comprised of father, mother and child. Auset would go on to be depicted as the Black Madonna in early European shrines, then later as the Virgin Mary in the Roman text. Heru is seen nowadays as the so-called Christ figure. The son, or shall I say, SUN in accordance with the winter solstice tradition, shining light to not only our will power over the figurative darkness, but also the Light of the Sun reborn each year as the days become longer (hence the December 25th birthday of Jesus). With this understanding we should also point out that the fallen angel of the bible (Satan, Lucifer, and the Devil), is merely the concept of us being controlled by or lower self, the emotions and ego as depicted by Set's reign over the kingdom in Ausar's defeat. Lastly, let's point out one other minor detail, it is the notion of Set killing his own brother, Ausar, which clearly has been rewritten as the story of Kane and Abel.

The story can also be found in the classic Disney film, "The Lion King." It's storyline nearly mirrors that of the story of Ausar perfectly. You have Ausar represented in Mufasa as the Father, Auset represented in Sarabi the Mother, Heru in Simba the son, and Set in the character Scar who takes the life of Mufasa in jealousy.

So, we see the story of Ausar has been revised and redistributed throughout the last 2,000 years in different variations but most notably as the story of Jesus. Though the hidden meanings may still be derived by those who have knowledge of the original tale, the significant difference is that teachings in the story of Jesus in no way alludes to the inner cultivation of self. Instead the teachings instruct its followers seek externally that which is internal, to await a messiah who will save only good Christians from "eternal damnation", and to fear Hell and it's Demons. When all along it is the Wisdom and Will power that saves us! Not from some lake of fire and a fire breathing devil but rather our own emotions, ego, and impulsive decisions! This has been a major blow to the spiritual development of a people. Specifically black people who were stripped of their true spiritual knowledge and forced into worshipping false idols painted to resemble the individuals that enslaved them. But by removing the wool from over the eyes of the sheep, the herd recognizes that they are their own shepherd and savior! Through this truth we may leave behind the mentality of fear and become free to walk in knowing our inner greatness as an Ausar resurrected!

It is important to understand that the life force within, the aforementioned "Chi" or "Ra", is depicted in this story as Ausar. The practice of mindfulness meditation turns our focus inwards to its presence and disciplines us to practice being mindful in our daily life. By becoming present in each moment and being mindful of our actions, we can thereby use our will and wisdom to not succumb to our impulses and emotions. Hence the resurrection of Ausar.

IV. The Eye of Heru and The Pineal Gland

The best and shortest road towards knowledge of truth is Nature. ~ Kemetic Axiom

A while back in the early part of my journey, a good friend reached out and asked me, "How do I unlock my Third Eye"? I would go on to explain that in order to do so you have to decalcify your Pineal Gland. This is a topic of great interest and importance so I decided to compound all the ways we can unlock our Third Eye into an easy 6 step guide anyone can follow.

First let me explain the relationship between the Third Eye and the Pineal Gland. The term "Third Eye" has its origins in the ancient civilizations of the Nile Valley. It originated from the ancient story of Ausar in which his son, Heru (or Horus) lost his eye in battle with Set. Now this is relevant because our ancestors used this story to explain natural phenomena in nature as well as our consciousness. In this case, the Pineal Gland was represented by the Eye of Heru to illustrate its spiritual faculties. You see the Pineal Gland is the energy center of our Brow Chakra, and it is closely connected to our use of clairvoyance and clairaudience, which is the ability to see and hear beyond the surface of things to extract its true meaning. Biologically, the Pineal Gland is light sensitive, and it reacts from sunlight to produce the hormone melatonin which regulates our sleep/wake cycle (circadian rhythm). There are many health benefits derived from Melatonin such as healthy eye sight, it's a natural anti-depressant, and it produces Melanin!

How does the Pineal Gland become calcified in the first place? A lack of sunlight, consumption of harmful chemicals, fluoride, excessive calcium and exposure to radiation all calcify the Pineal Gland. Over time the gland begins to harden, preventing its ability to release melatonin. That said lets jump right into the 6 steps to decalcify the Pineal Gland and unlock your Third Eye!

1. GET SOME SUN! Adults should get 2 hours of sunlight per day, children 30 minutes. (Those with lighter pigmentation are recommended lesser amounts or to use sunscreen. Melatonin supplements are available to combat the deficiency). Sungazing is a great way to consume the sunlight! During sunrise and sunset, the UV index is much lower and we are able to look directly into the Suns glow without harming our eyes.

2. EAT TO LIVE! Eating a whole food, plant based diet is one of the fastest ways to unlocking your Third Eye! Dark leafy greens, which receive their pigmentation from the

sunlight through chlorophyll, are packed with melanin and by consuming them we increase our levels of this vital molecule! Here are 3 foods to add to your diet right away to decalcify your pineal gland: I) Seaweed. Seaweed is packed with iodine which removes fluoride, making seaweed a potent food for decalcifying the Pineal Gland. II) Watercress. Watercress is another dark green packed with iodine and is also known to fight off cancer cells! III) Bananas. Bananas are rich with the amino acid tryptophan which aides in the production of melatonin.

3. DON'T DRINK TAP WATER! The mineral Fluoride is intentionally added to tap water due to its ability to help prevent tooth decay. The problem, as mentioned before, is that fluoride hardens the pineal gland and interferes with our natural hormonal cycles. Most toothpastes also contain fluoride for the same reasoning, however there are natural toothpaste's available with natural alternatives to fluoride to boost healthy oral hygiene.

4. CRYSTALS! Crystals have been used since ancient times for their healing and spiritual properties. Each crystal has its own unique properties. For example, you can use a Smoky Quartz Crystal to protect your pineal gland from the excessive radiation of computers, laptops and cellphones, then in turn use a Fluorite Quartz to enhance the Third Eye!

5. MEDITATION! Meditation will activate your Third Eye in a tremendous way! By

submerging yourself into the present moment and becoming aware of all that you are feeling internally, you will develop your sense of clairvoyance and clairaudience. You will begin to notice premonitions and signs the universe is sending your way. This will allow you to begin creating the reality you desire!

6. READ MORE! Read to expand your consciousness! The saying is that knowledge is power. I personally think the restriction of knowledge gives power to those concealing the information. All the secrets are recorded in a book somewhere. But at the same time, question EVERYTHING. What I mean by that is if what you are reading, watching and hearing serves no purpose in elevating your life, then simply let it go. Often times people take what is written in text as fact, when in actuality it is just the beliefs of one person expressed in written form. Dive into content that will give value to your life. Find books that help bring out the light you hold within.

Those are all great steps to take in decalcifying the pineal gland and opening your third eye. But how do you know if it's working? How will you know that the changes to your lifestyle are having any sort of positive outcome? Well allow me to explain what I have experienced once I made these changes.

A huge sign that your third eye is open is you begin to have a heightened sense of intuition. Ever noticed how women seem to have a high level of intuition almost effortlessly? This is why in ancient times the oracles were mostly female. In ancient Kemet women were viewed as equals to men and took on roles such as priestess and Pharaoh. The first known human was a woman. The energy of the planet is feminine (more on this in chapter 7 where I discuss Earthing). You see where I'm going here? Women naturally possess a high level of intuition, in my opinion, due to their close connection with Mother Earth. Getting more sun, eating plant based, the use of crystals and meditation are all steps that will strengthen your connection with the planet and heighten your intuition.

When your third eye is open you recognize patterns and understand what will take place in a given circumstance based on past experiences. If you are someone who hears a news story and things aren't adding up, you see there are missing pieces to what is being presented to you, that's another huge sign your third eye is open. You search for the deeper truth behind the story and take into consideration things like what industries, government or sponsoring businesses would hold a financial interest in the topic.

Once you've stopped eating meat and animal products for about a good two months, you will really begin to notice that your third eye is opening. This because embedded in food is information! When you are eating from Mother Earth you are simultaneously downloading information on a cellular level that will reconnect you with nature. How so? Well the organs in our body create new cells at varying rates. By cutting out meats, dairy and foods that cause harm to the body and replacing them with fruits, vegetables and foods grown from the earth, we are fueling the growth of new cells with energy from the Earth and Sun. What we eat we become and after a good month or two of eating plant based you will begin to feel your connection with the planet on an internal level.

The last great sign your third eye is open and you've activated your pineal gland is this: You see people beyond their physical nature. Without them even saying one word you feel their aura and you sense their energy. This is why young children are so special. You see they have not yet been diluted with the ways of society, and just the energy a person carries in their presence can bring them joy and excitement (or the other way around).

You can choose not to open your third eye and decalcify your pineal gland for the sake of carrying on with life as it has been. Or you can start making the aforementioned adjustments, continue reading this text, and discover your power that lies within.

V. The 7 Hermetic Principles of Tehuti

All cognition comes from within; we are initiated only by ourselves, but the Master gives the keys. ~ Kemetic Axiom

From ancient Kemet we've received the fundamental occult teachings that have brought about higher wisdom throughout all nations and peoples for the last 20,000 years. All nations have borrowed from the ancient African teachings of the Nile Valley; India, China, Greece, Rome and of course the so-called "modern" western world.

In ancient Kemet resided "The Master of Masters." Deified as the God of Wisdom, he was known as Tehuti. After the Greeks invaded the land of Kemet under the direction of Alexander the Great, he was renamed as "Thoth" and later once introduced to the European continent, he was given the name "Hermes Trismegistus" meaning the "thrice-great". Out of respect to the original African teachings before European invasion, I will refer to him as Tehuti, the deity of wisdom.

Long before today's modern sciences there was the ancient African Spiritual Science. What the ancients knew then is being proven today in the works of Quantum Physics. These 7 principles, universal laws if you will, can be used to describe the natural phenomena and forces of the physical world. But what is most enlightening and useful to the growth of human kind, is the duel relation to our own conscious and subconscious occurrences. Let's dive on into the 7 Hermetic Principles of Tehuti!

1. MENTALISM: The first principle is based on the truth that "All is Mind". In this context the word "All" is being used to describe things seen and knowable in reality and in nature. This principle embodies the truth that the miracle of Life, Energy, Matter and all that we are able to experience with our senses is SPIRIT. Spirit being unseen and unknowable, yet beneath the surface of things it may be considered as the infinite mind of the universe to which we are all connected. This principle plays out within the inner workings of our own body at every

moment. The Omniscience of our life force energy, which operates our heartbeat, metabolism, insulin, and etc. all within our subconscious mind where we are bound connected to the infinite mind of ALL.

2. CORRESPONDENCE: As above, so below; as below, so above; as within, so without. The second principle uncovers the hidden truth that the universal laws and natural phenomena operate on every plane of existence. The ancients held such mastery of this principle that they illustrated it through the greatest work of architecture known to mankind. The three great Pyramids of Giza in which they were aligned perfectly to the stars of Orion's Belt! As above so below. The human body is composed of the same natural elements as the stars of the universe. More significantly, the omnipotent life force energy maintaining our atoms within, also controls the planets, galaxies and stars without. As above, so below; as within, so without.

3. VIBRATION: A great truth, the third principle of vibration. Modern physics has long endorsed this truth that everything is in motion. So many scientific accounts that verify this truth, yet it is one known to the ancients thousands of years before the scientific method would ever be used. Energy which is purely vibrations, can never be destroyed only transferred. Combine this principle with that of Correspondence and it

becomes violently visible that what we eat has a profound effect on our experience. The dead energy of a tortured corps as opposed to the live enzymes and high electric conductivity of fresh fruits, it is apparent which of these foods will raise the vibrations of the individual (As within so without). Perhaps the most intriguing part of this principle is the knowledge that just as everything vibrates on the physical plane, so too does everything vibrate on the mental plane. The masters of ancient Kemet and the masters of today know that Knowledge is Power (the first principle of Mentalism), and that by raising one's mental vibrations and through the use of our will power, we can reproduce our mental energy in the minds of others. The same way color can be reproduced by vibrations light, we can reproduce the mental state of others as we see fit by having their mind vibrate at the appropriate level. ALL is mental.

4. POLARITY: Fire, water; Hot, cold; Yin, yang etc. Everything has its opposite. More importantly we recognize with this principle that opposites are actually identical in nature, just vibrating at opposite levels. In fact all opposites can be brought together. Let's take love and hate for example, the two are opposites on the pole of emotion, but if we take two individuals we love, and say we love one individual slightly more than we love the other, then we can imply we hate the lesser of the two slightly more than the other. This holds true for

hot and cold, like and dislike, and my favorite to observe being Democrat and Republican. The function of Government being to regulate what is "allowed" or "not allowed" by the public, to varying degrees, these two forms of government are the same in nature only different in degree. If the "choice" presented to us is simply a degree on the scale of the same system, was there ever really a choice?

5. RHYTHM: Yes the principle that everything flows. The pendulum swing manifests itself on all levels through any given type of thing as described in the principle of polarity. The pendulum will swing from the bitter cold of January to the hot days of July, or vice versa depending on which hemisphere of the planet you're on. Like all others, this law also manifests in the mental states of our consciousness. The masters of old knew that by again applying the WILL, they could not escape this law but they could counterbalance its effects. What I mean by that is this; Rather than being slaves to the emotions which swing along the pendulum from say angry to happy, the ancients used mental alchemy (also referred to as mental transmutation) to rise above this law and vibrate at the desired state. Every day we see those who are slaves to their emotions and the swing of the pendulum, but the true Millennial Initiate consciously holds a level of mental control that, let's face it, many just cannot comprehend.

6. CAUSE AND EFFECT: Have you ever considered the trillions of events that have taken place just for you to be here right now breathing! The birth of our Sun, Mother Earth, the countless chemical reactions to spark life, millions of years all leading to the day you were born! Every Cause has its Effect; Every Effect has its Cause. There is no such thing as coincidence. Everything has happened, and is happening in order of cause and effect. So to is law on the mental plane. Those who have mastered this law use it to their advantage. While the masses are swept up in cause and effect like a ping pong ball simply reacting to the impact felt, the Millennial Initiate will use this principle and plant seeds. They understand that seeds planted today will bear fruit for tomorrow. This principle exemplifies the game of Life! "The Future is an Open Book for Those Who Can Read" - Tehuti (Translated by M. Doreal, The Emerald Tablets of Thoth The Atlantean, Revised, 2006).

7. GENDER – Ah yes, the great principle of Gender. Not only in the sexes of species (male/female), but more importantly in the protons and electrons that exist in all things! Nothing could ever exist without this principle. The omnipresence of every atom, which are the building blocks of the material world, exists only by the combination of positive and negative energies (protons and neutrons). Life

in our species can only exist by the principle of gender. Like each of the other principles, this principle also manifests itself in the mental plane. It is what the ancients referred to as the Divine Masculine and Divine Feminine. Illustrated in hieroglyphs as Khepri, a scarab beetle, whose left side represents the Divine Masculine and right side represents the Divine Feminine, it is symbolic of the human brain! The masculine energy of the left side being ever progressive, and able to view the parts of a thing systemically. It is the function of your mind able to break down each letter and word in this sentence. All the while the Divine Feminine, the right side of the brain existing to combine the sum into a whole. It is also the creative side of the brain which the ancients used so heavily in their ability to create and decipher pictograms with dual, sometimes triple meaning. This knowledge and utilization of such advance psychology tens of thousands of years ago begs the question, are we really so modern or have we back tracked and become a primitive species?

These are some heavy concepts to take in when first introduced. Take some time to internalize them. Then apply them in your everyday life and discover just how much power you hold!

When I think about the forgotten knowledge of the ancient Kemetic civilization, these 7 principles first come to mind. For a moment just imagine what we as a collective can accomplish if we live knowing our interconnectedness at the level of the subconscious mind, the universal mind. Knowing that our subconscious mind is the same supercomputer regulating the orbit of galaxies, vibrating in every atom of what we see physically. What if each of us internalized the law of causation? Recognizing that on greater planes of existence planets are born through chemical cause and effect, but right here on our own level we can shape our own world using this same principle. Then use the principle of gender to impregnate our subconscious mind with thoughts, ideas and possibilities so that our internal supercomputer may birth those ideas into reality!

VI. Removing the Wool

You will free yourself when you learn to be neutral and follow your heart without letting things sway you. ~ Kemetic Axiom

We have now taken into account the ancient views on spirit, the scientific expression of subconscious mind, and the Hermetic truth that everything vibrates and therefore is energy. Using that background we can now clearly identify the forces being used against mankind in this long lasting spiritual warfare. They are hidden in plain sight for those with eyes to see, if we first remove the wool from over the eyes of the sheep.

But how has this come to pass in our own people? How could we as descendants of the greatest civilizations to have walked the earth, find ourselves living in a system created to harness our own energy for the gain of its creators. Everything starts at the level of spirit, the subconscious and beliefs. Therefore we have to objectively examine the events in which religion was weaponized as a tool of mental and spiritual enslavement. "To win a people for Christ, it is necessary to Europeanize them. Behind all systems of administration lies the fundamental question of what we intend to make of the African?" (Edwin Smith, The Golden Stool, 1927). Unfortunately this question has been answered in several ways. The greatest example being through the use of tyranny. The most effective tool that was, and is still being used to do this is the religion that was forced upon our African Ancestors. This religion is CHRISTIANITY! A sad truth when I give notice to the presence of thousands of ancestors, whose energy lives on through my DNA, knowing that they were conquered physically, mentally and spiritually in the name of Jesus. Smith, the author quoted in the passage, was a missionary working in the continent of Africa. Later in the same book he would go on to state: "The first method is to destroy their institutions, tradition, religions, and habits of the people and then superimpose upon the ruins whatever the governing power considers to be a better administration system. The other methods (while checking the worst abuses) tries to graft our higher civilization on the soundly rooted native stock, bringing out the best of what is in the native tradition and molding it into a form consonant with our modern ideas and higher standards. Since a civilization is the expression of the mind of a people the African must first be endowed with a European mind if he is to be civilized." (Edwin Smith, The Golden Stool, 1927).

Pure evil, clearly. So much of what we may have thought we knew, what we were programmed to believe, has been a lie. The result has been generation upon generation where as a collective we lost sight of the power we hold, and instead we externalized our power to a false deity. Remember, the Spiritual Warfare that is going on starts within! But through wisdom and will, we may overthrow any restraining beliefs!

Freedom is every person's birth right and dogmatic religion is just one of many tools being used to restrict that right. It has unfortunately become a reality that the majority of people are slaves within their own mind and therefore slaves on the physical plane of existence as well (as within, so without). Unknowingly, by deception they have allowed themselves to be manipulated by the WILL of others, yet believing themselves to be "free" and able to make choices of their own. Now wrap your mind around this, are choices really a faculty of freedom if the options presented were never your own? Let's take for instance the U.S. political system. Far too often individuals get wrapped up in the sway of politics, believing they are making an educated decision to vote in order with a particular political party. What the Law of polarity illuminates is that all opposites are the same in nature, varying only in degree. So with that in mind, we must recognize that Democrats and Republicans are merely opposing ends of the same stick! Would you not say that the fundamental purpose of government is to wield a degree of control over the public? Whether liberal or conservative the idea and function of government remains the same. To enact policies and regulations that are in line with the controlling parties constituents. Though we are all interconnected spiritually and in the field of energy, we each are living out our own human experience. That in mind, there will always be aspects of government that are in opposition to our core needs and values. Subjecting ourselves to such a thing is actually parallel to relying on a deity for our saving. It is again focusing on the external when our attention should center on what we can control. A great way to do this is by using the circle in a circle method.

    In your mind (or on paper) I want you to draw a circle. Now in that circle represents everything within your control; your emotions, habits, what you consume and etc. Now outside of that circle I want you to draw a much larger circle. This exterior circle represents all of the things that go on around you that you do not have direct control over. In your day to day try and keep in mind that what's in the interior circle, what you can control is what you should act upon. The exterior circle we have no control over, thus we should remain very guarded in what we allow to penetrate our interior circle and influence our emotions, habits and actions. Now as the events external of us take place, we must navigate our interior circle through the storms of the exterior, but never losing control of those interior faculties.

    Keeping the circle principle in mind, now take into account that the most effective tool that can be used to impress upon ones subconscious mind is imagery. With the subconscious mind regulating 95% of our actions independent from conscious thought, it behooves us to filter the images we take in. Imagery, when used to reprogram the mind on an objective is actually very effective. A bit of present day irony as it relates to subconscious influence is that we've been spooked away from practices like the use of crystals, sage, and natural substances of the Earth, having been told that they are taboo and witchcraft, yet if we look at the tactics used by big businesses and government alike, it turns out that they are actually the biggest witch doctors of all!

The definition of "magick" is "The science and art of causing change to occur in conformity with WILL" (Aleister Crowley, The Book of the Law, 1904). Remember, all is energy and imagery is the best method to influence the subconscious. So when we think of things such as magic and spells what we are actually dealing with are techniques to alter one's perception, or impress something onto their subconscious mind. Most people think of show magic, sleight of hand, or some mystical prowess when you bring up magic. That in itself is an illusion! All the while, REAL magic is at work every single day. In fact I'm sure a great many of you work in professions where the very objective of your work is to conduct actual magic. Marketing, advertising, sales, broadcasting, writing and even public speech are methods used to convey thoughts and if applied strategically, will alter the perception of an individual.

You don't want to spend an entire lifespan caught living under the spell of someone else's WILL. Organizations prey on our emotions knowing that most of the time we are not being mindful of what we are experiencing, thus we act on impulse to what has been presented to our perception. Perception shapes our perspective, which molds our belief systems, thus our thinking. We must be very selective in what we consume visually and in audible, otherwise our psyche may quickly fall victim to this sort of thing. Never forget the conquest of Set, usurping the kingdom of Ausar within.

Be mindful of the sensations you feel from mass media and advertisements. Every week there is a new bombshell in the news media. When it happens, be mindful of what you are feeling and how the topic triggered certain impulses within you. The same goes with advertisements and marketing efforts. Their objective is to stir some form of emotion within you, then provide a solution for that emotion. Ever notice those commercials showing a starving child somewhere in the world? This is not a gripe towards any group of people living as victims to an unjust system to which I spit upon, however stay with me as I extract a point here. Those commercials often have a somber audio playing in the background coupled with some of the most disturbing imagery you have ever seen. They then provide you with a feel good option, a solution for the emotion that has riled up inside of you. Set up a plan today to send money and sponsor a child here. In that moment, your perception says "I must act!", but have we considered all angles of the scenario? The imagery and audio was created in a very deliberate way to influence how you see the situation. Sure, unfortunately there are children starving and families living in poverty both domestically and abroad, but let's first consider who the organization is that has asked for your donation. Does the money actually end up with the families or is it used to fund experimental vaccinations amongst other things, exploiting an already vulnerable group. Further, has this intense imagery given you the viewer a completely false impression of a nation, creating a negative stigma on an area or people you actually have no experience with! That's just one example.

There is also a bit of unspoken history regarding the use of imagery in film. An unspoken ritualistic tradition that lies behind the making of Hollywood. Now we've all heard the "Illuminati" conspiracy theories as it relates to this industry, I am in no way confirming or denying the existence of such, but I want to be clear that those theorics are not what I am referring to. What I am more concerned with sharing are the ancient rituals that may have inspired so much of the origin of film in this country. So much so that they are placed right in plain sight, embedded in the very name "Hollywood".

In ancient Europe, there was a sect of people known as the Druids. These were a select group of high ranking Christian leaders, Judges and medical professionals etc. The Druids would use wood from the Holly tree to create wands that they would then use to cast spells. Now at first read you may think of this as a silly thing, wondering "how can a tree branch actually be used for such a thing?" But remember, everything is energy! Just as certain herbs and vegetables bare healing properties, there are natural resources on this Earth that hold certain energetic properties. Sandalwood for example is known to enhance one's clairvoyance, while Quartz crystals are said to hold properties in which they absorb negative energy (based on ancient tradition and research conducted by Dr. Marcel Vogel). If used with knowledge of said properties they can do wonders. In the case of the Holly and its use by the Druids, they are said to have used it for dream work by ritualistic means. By invoking the Holly's energy they would influence ones subconscious. Ironically enough, actors in Hollywood productions are termed a "cast". In fact, that area of California is known to bare an abundance of Holly trees. Furthermore, the reefs & mistletoe that hang during the pagan Christmas holiday are also from the Holly tree. Coincidental? I think not, as discussed there are no coincidences in our existence. Every cause has its effect, and every effect its cause. This is the very magic used by the movie makers of Hollywood. William Shakespeare is quoted as once saying "All the world is a stage, and all the men and women merely players" (William Shakespeare, As You Like It, 1603).

Recognize the extent businesses, media & government will go to in order to influence your mental perception. Your mind holds so much value and if left unguarded it will be manipulated by those who understand how to deceive it. Even on an interpersonal level, become conscious of the influence others may hold upon you. Have you ever taken the time to actually pay attention to the mood others are in around you, and how their mood then makes you feel? If someone in your proximity is exuding happiness, it may likely have a positive effect on your state of mind. These are the types of people you want to keep in your circle.

So you see, when we begin to understand and identify less with our persona and more with that 95% subconscious life force, the spiritual warfare all around us becomes apparent. By first being able to see beyond illusion, and recognizing what is being done by others to gain an influence on your subconscious, we can then work towards protecting that energy. Understand and know just how much power you hold over your emotions, ego, cravings & sensations. Things we often identify with (brands, political view, religion, foods, even race etc.) are all triggers to those faculties but they are not set in stone. You can re-program your belief systems to what better serves you and the path you want in life! In fact, it behooves each of us no matter how far along we are in our journey, to periodically take notice of our belief systems and question their authenticity. By paying attention to those feelings and noticing the triggers as they happen we can begin to exercise our WILL power over them. Remember, all is mental!

VII.   Mindfulness Meditation

Knowledge is consciousness of reality. Reality is the sum of the laws governing nature and the causes from which they flow. ~ Kemetic Axiom

From here forward we are transitioning from knowledge to application. Best practices to use the aforementioned subjects into our daily lives. Because we grew up with many of these belief systems, behaviors and traditions, it is a massive undertaking for the mind to de-program itself from all that has been put in. If you wanted to transform your body you wouldn't go to the gym after a long hiatus and attempt to bench press 300 pounds, at least I hope not. You would start exercising, working out to build yourself up to where you want to be. This is exactly what we must do with our mind. Our brain functions and works like any other muscle in the body, in that the more you use it the stronger it becomes. Mindfulness meditation is a great practice for strengthening the mind to recognize what we feel in the given moment.

Before diving heavily into the practice of mindfulness itself, I find it appropriate to cover the origins of modern yoga, Hinduism, and mindfulness. The spiritual practices of the ancient Nile Valley civilizations didn't just suddenly vanish only to be rediscovered in the 21st century. They were first carried on to southern India by migrants from east Africa who would go on to become known as the Dravidian people of India. The Aryan people of the north invaded the land of the Dravidians and outlawed their religious and spiritual traditions. This resulted in the spiritual practices of the blacks being nearly torn to pieces with portions being integrated with the religion of the invading Aryans, birthing modern Hinduism. A breadcrumb left behind in the connection lies in the Goddess Tara whose characteristics seem to blend that of Ausar and Auset. I find that even amongst spiritual, more "conscious" circles, this is a truth not very well known or talked about. So having briefly touched on the Dravidian civilization, this beacon of light in the east from whom so much of today's spiritual practices in Hinduism and subsequently Buddhism can be attributed, lets dive into the inner workings of mindfulness.

Mindfulness meditation can take place anywhere. In a perfect world we would all practice somewhere in a nature space, amongst greenery, under the sun, or out on the beach. Somewhere where we can embrace our oneness with the Earth. That's great in a perfect world but for those of us who live in or near a city space, we have to find other ways to bring about a natural state of being. Not all of us are lucky enough to have the beach in our backyard, however; with a little imagination and a few essentials we can transform even the smallest of spaces into a mellow meditation station. Let's say you live in an apartment, the first thing you want to do is find a space away from the distraction of kids or roommates, whatever the case may be. Hopefully you find a space with some natural lighting but it's not a must have. Next, you'll want a comfy pillow or chair. Something you can sit or kneel on and have good posture which will promote a good airflow in the breathing. Lastly, if you can, try and add some natural soothing sensations using things like incense for aromatherapy, nature sounds or subtle imagery. That quickly you've created a meditation space without having to struggle with finding a setting.

What I have come to find along my journey is that the beauty of mindfulness is that it all takes place within. You don't have to go anywhere to meditate you just need to simply return your consciousness to yourself and away from the external. Of course some conditions are more ideal than others, but the whole point of mindfulness is to become fully aware of what you are feeling internally and externally. With that said, it does not matter if you're sitting in your car in a parking lot outside of your job, or at the park with the sounds of nature. The act of paying attention to what you feel inside is a one person sport!

Typically, time is the number 1 reason as to why we don't accomplish all that we know we should be doing. But you see time is an illusion, we can't live in the past or future, we have right now! It doesn't take much time to meditate, all it takes is conscious awareness. Every minute of every day we have a choice, remember from the universal law of cause and effect that we can use or WILL to plant seeds today for what we want tomorrow. So we will either choose to make time now to better our overall health and wellness, or we will be forced to give our time later as a result. At this point there has been a lot mentioned as to what we should be mindful of, and the need to strengthen the mind using meditation, so here is an easy to follow, quick 5 minute meditation guide that anyone can do just about anywhere.

1. Gather yourself into a comfortable position. You may be sitting, lying down or even walking or driving. The beauty of mindfulness meditation is that the focus is all mental and internal therefore it can be accomplished while doing most activities. I even enjoy practicing mindfulness while folding laundry.

2. If you are seated you should compose yourself and get into a comfortable posture. Close your eyes if you can as it will help you to connect with your inner self. If you are walking begin to enter a natural pace, not very hasty as you are in no rush when being mindful. Remember it is about become present in the moment, not rushing to get to next experience.

3. Become aware of what you are feeling. Begin to focus on what is going on with your body, notice the subtle vibrations within your

extremities, the heart beat and any tingling sensations within.

4. Breathe in and breathe out. Start to give attention to your breathing, inhale that life force energy deep down into your lower abdomen. Notice how you feel internally as the prana seeps in from your mouth, down into your chest and eventually arriving at the lower abdomen. Pause for just a few seconds at the height of the inhale, then slowly exhale and notice the sensations in the body such as the deflation of the stomach. Now you are present in the moment, as you pay attention to the breathing cycle and your sensations within, your mind has its anchor. Not anticipating the next breath, or reliving the last, but focused mindfully on the current inhale and exhale. What I like to do is inhale for 5 seconds, hold it for 6 seconds, and then slowly release for 8 seconds.

5. The mind will wander. At some point your mind will drift and you'll lose focus of the breath. Thoughts, daydreams, cravings or memories will begin to flow through and this is perfectly FINE. This doesn't mean you failed at meditating, this is just simply what our minds do. When you notice that this has happened, give yourself a mental pat on the back and congratulate yourself! By noticing the drift you have become aware and are able to easily refocus yourself to your breathing.

6. Continue with this practice for about 5 minutes or so, even longer if you like. As you go along

remember to use your breathing as an anchor, and when you notice your mind wandering remember that it is a positive because you were able to recognize what you have experienced. Then lightly return to your breathing and embrace the life force energy flowing through you.

I find step 5 to be the most significant step in mindfulness for me personally. You may agree, especially if you are someone who seems to have never ending thoughts racing through your mind. We have to remember that it's not about trying to "shut up" that busy brain, but rather becoming present and aware of those thoughts, recognizing what we are feeling and allowing it to flow right out of your mind just as easy as it came in. By doing so you are strengthening your mental to overcome the grip of any mind state that may not be in your best interest. When we strap that mind down to a single task like breathing, it becomes easy to highlight and remove the distractions entering our brain. You start to notice that even when you're going about your day to day actions you will catch yourself when your mind is drifting. This becomes extremely useful in overcoming impulses and emotional decisions.

Sometimes the best way for us to become more mindful is by objectively asking ourselves questions that will bring our focus to what we are experiencing internally. There is an ancient Kemetic proverb that reads "An answer brings no illumination unless the question has matured to give rise to this answer. Therefore learn how to put a question." (Ihsa Schwaller de Lubics, Her-Bak: The Living Face of Ancient Egypt, 1978). That is powerful! Often times our most enlightened moments come not from being told a statement, rather pondering an answer leading to an "aha" moment.

Once we are aware of our thoughts and what type of external influences programmed such thinking, we are able to make the mental corrections for the desired outcome. Sometimes, in order to even bring our awareness to the influences in the first place, we have to ask ourselves thought provoking, mindful questions. We often see the phrase "thoughts become words and words become actions", but there is a science behind this. For over a century neuroscientists have been studying the phenomena called "neuroplasticity", which is the brains ability to become stronger at what it is most often tasked. What we do most our brain will master and if it is routine it will become our reality. With our livelihood riding on the reality shaped in our brain, have we even taken note of what's going on in our mind to begin with?

Here are 6 great questions with some example answers to cultivate mindfulness!

1. Are these thoughts and actions serving me? A) Yes, my thoughts and actions are in tune with what I want out of life. If not, then no; my thoughts and actions are not in harmony with what I choose for my life, therefore I will reprogram my thinking (see numbers 5 & 6).

2. How can I add value to society? A) I can give a compliment, a warm greeting and put out good energy. If I pay close attention, I can find a need that I can fill by providing a service or goods.

3. What am I grateful for? A) I am grateful for the air that flows through my lungs, the life force keeping my heart beat and the cognitive functions allowing me to discern and make sound judgement.

4. Where are my emotions right now? A) I am aware of my emotions and I choose whether or not I will act upon them. I am not a slave to my emotions. Rather, I remain the master and they remain the servant!

5. What are my thoughts and what shaped them? A) My thoughts, beliefs and opinions are a direct result of my mental programs. I am responsible for those programs and able to adjust them accordingly.

6. What is my goal and how can I program my brain to achieving it? A) My goal is ___ and through repetition, imagery and sound I am able to program my mind in achieving this goal.

It is by no means a one size fits all so I encourage you to take the basis of the information and apply it in a way that seems best for you. Stick with it, realize the benefits then pay it forward to someone else. Remember, we are not slaves to our emotions but rather masters of them!

Living a more mindful lifestyle can go a long way in improving our interactions in this modern world where smartphones, tablets and all sorts of technology seem to have taken over. Mindfulness is also a great way to become more aware of our device usage and actively create habits to use technology in a more productive manner. When we absorb ourselves into the present moment and really pay attention to how often our hands naturally want to reach into our pockets for a smartphone, it becomes very eye-opening just how addicted we are. Here are a couple different ways to become mindful of your device usage.

- Organized Planning

Ever tried planning your days from start to finish? Of course there are many variables and unexpected events so it's tough to say 100% how your day will flow. But start with the essentials: Your sleep time, work or school, exercise and meal time. Then start adding your time for investing in yourself: Reading, hobbies, time with friends, meditation and planning. Once you've done all this, then you can objectively see how much time you have for your devices.

- Non-Negotiables

Now that we have our schedule, we must establish some non-negotiables with ourselves to become consciously aware of what we are doing throughout the day. This way we can hold ourselves accountable so that we don't fall to the urge to dive right back into our devices. A great way to start is by turning off notifications for any unneeded apps. Facebook, Instagram and that game you love can all wait. Set family guidelines as to when it will be TV or game time. When out or in with others, make it a point to put your phone on silent, or in another room. Avoid mindlessly staring at your phone as you walk down the street or the hallways at school or work. We often shrug off strangers when we do this and in turn we miss out on what could be great conversations and opportunities to grow and help one another.

   There we have it! We've become aware of our connection with the devices, we've created a daily log and set boundaries to guide our usage, now let's add in this mindfulness exercise to detach from impulsive device usage.

1. Whenever your phone rings, pings or vibrates, first gather yourself and take a breath. Before you touch it ask yourself, can it wait? Then decide what to do, remembering the device is your servant not the other way around!

2. If you've started down a mindless binge, catch yourself! The same way we catch our mind wandering with the mindful meditation, apply the same principle here. You clicked a link, then another, or your speeding through text messages left and right, just typing away. Start becoming aware of these types of habits and work on catching yourself sooner and sooner. Notice how what you are looking at effects you emotionally, and its influence on your thoughts.

3. When you've managed to catch yourself zoned out into your phone, take a deep breath and realize that in this moment you can be engaged in something productive that you previously mapped out for your day.

   Every now and then a detox from our devices is necessary, but becoming more mindful on a daily basis may be the more practical route. There are so many advantages afforded to us by technology, so much so that when used strategically we can change our lives and leave a lasting impact on the world. Remember, technology is here to serve us and not the other way around.

Earthing, or grounding, is another form of meditation I highly recommend. When was the last time you grounded yourself by placing your bare feet on Gaia, Mother Earth? This is what's referred to as "earthing" and it has tremendous health benefits. That's right, by simply walking barefoot on soil, grass or sand at the beach, you are doing your body a great service! There is a science behind grounding. When we are in good health our body's electricity is at about a neutral state. However, when you are carrying disease or rather "dis-ease", your body is producing lots of inflammation and mucus, resulting in part from excessive positive ions. The surface of earth is packed with tons of antioxidants and negative ions, thus when we place our body on the surface we are balancing and healing ourselves in a very natural way.

What science has proven and what the ancients have known for thousands of years is that ALL is Energy. Every cell, every atom of matter is purely vibrations of energy (remember the 3rd Hermetic principle of vibration). So when we are off physically, mentally and emotionally it is because something within is out of balance. We aren't vibrating in a cohesive manner, our energy is misfiring. "More than 5000 scientific documents based on research in Israel, Europe, and the Orient; support the concept that high doses of negative ions have positive effect while opposite is true with exposure to high amounts of positive ions" (Denise Mann, Negative ions create positive vibes. WebMD Feature, 2012). "It is an established, though not widely appreciated fact, that the Earth's surface possesses a limitless and continuously renewed supply of free or mobile electrons" (Gaetan Chavalier, Earthing: Health Implications of Reconnecting the Human Body to the Earth's Surface Electrons. Journal of Environmental and Public Health, 2012 Retrieved from https://www.ncbi.nlm.nih.gov/pmc/articles/PMC3265077/.).

By balancing the negative and positive subatomic energy inside of us, we are reducing anxiety, enhancing our immune system, improving digestion, balancing the nervous system, enhancing memory and improving our sleep. To be specific; Arthritis, cancer, high blood pressure, tuberculosis, Pneumonia, depression, allergies, asthma and rage are just some of the many forms of dis-ease that negative ions from earth can be used to treat and improve health.

For me personally, grounding reinforces my understanding of the oneness with all. It's a spiritual experience reminding me that everything is connected, which is the secret of the universe. I practice earthing for just a few minutes each day in combination with mindfulness. It allows me to connect with my higher self, remembering that the divine is all around, within, and through me. Thus I'm able to become my greatest version and walk in the light of my inner being. There is an old Native American proverb that says "It is not the land that belongs to you, it is you that belong to the land".

A quick recap because there's a lot of value in this chapter. We've briefly covered the untold origins of spiritual practices in the Indus Valley and the connection to black people. How to set up a meditation space and create a natural environment even in the heart of the city. We've gone through a 6 step mindfulness exercise and identified the types of questions we can ask ourselves to bring internal focus. We even covered how we can become mindful in our use of technology and broke down the science of Earthing! This chapter can be a valuable resource and great starting point for anyone serious about leading a more mindful lifestyle. When we think of the ancient teachings of Kemet and the spiritual work of old, the techniques covered are definitely a 21st century hack into riving the spirit of the ancestors. The power rests within each of us in the present moment. But it gets even better when we combine mindfulness with what we put in our body!

VIII.   Eat To Live

The body is the house of the divine, therefore it is said "Know Thyself". ~Kemetic Axiom

The late great Dr. Sebi once said "Mucus is the cause of disease in the body". Sebi coined what is referred to as the Alkaline diet, as a way of ridding the body of all disease. The alkaline diet is all about restoring an environment within the body where disease cannot thrive. A common misconception is that eating alkaline food is about making your body more alkaline when in actuality the goal is to support your body in returning to its own natural pH balance. You see, it's not that we need to become more alkaline, it's that we've become too acidic which I will explain. Mucus is our body's natural defense mechanism against external bacteria however; when there is an excess of mucus disease will form. Take Bronchitis for instance. This disease is a result of excessive mucus in the bronchial tubes. The same is true with Pneumonia and mucus in the lungs, or Arthritis and mucus in the joints. The question then is how does all this excessive mucus build up in the first place? The short answer, an ACIDIC lifestyle!

The body's natural pH level is about 7.365. When you live an acidic lifestyle the body has to work extremely hard to maintain this pH 7.365. What's an "Acidic lifestyle"? Consuming foods and drinks with a pH level way below the body's natural range, no exercise, lots of alcohol, cigarettes, sweets, sugars, yeasts etc.. The goal in eating more alkaline foods is to support the natural pH level of our body which will in turn help us to prevent and in some cases reverse disease. As Hippocrates once said, "Let food be thy medicine and medicine be thy food"!

There are levels when it comes to Eating to Live. A good entry level for some would be a Pescetarian diet. These are people who do not consume any meat outside of seafood. You then have Vegetarians, who do not consume any meat at all, however they do consume dairy products. The next tier would be Vegans. This group does not consume any meat or dairy products. They also refrain from wearing any clothing or using any products derived from animals, however they do consume processed foods so long as there are no animal contents. Things turn up even more after the level of vegan. You have Plant-Based vegans who only consume products derived from fruits and vegetables, Fruitarians who only consume fruits, and lastly the Alkaline Vegan. Similar to the vegan diet in that it prohibits the consumption of meat and dairy, those on an alkaline diet also refrain from acidic foods that promote disease. These things include alcohol, coffee, some grains and even high acidic fruits and vegetables. You may be wondering, well what do alkaline vegans eat? Well with over 20,000 edible plant species in the world there is plenty to choose from. In fact, here are my 5 top alkaline foods that everyone should be incorporating into their diet!

1. Spinach- Most leafy greens are alkaline, but there is just something extra special about spinach. Even most people who don't really care for greens typically enjoy spinach because of its mild flavor. Spinach is exceptionally rich in vitamin K, vitamin A, manganese, magnesium and so much more! Studies show that just one cup of spinach in your daily diet will aid in digestion, prevent constipation, maintain blood sugar, and even help curb your appetite if you are trying to lose weight!

2. Avocados: This super-food is both nutrient dense and delicious! Avocados contain lots of healthy fats, specifically Oleic acid which studies show to be very beneficial in fighting cancer. In addition to being alkaline, anti-inflammatory and heart healthy, this alkaline favorite even holds a higher concentration of potassium than bananas! Potassium has been shown to lower blood pressure which aids in fighting off stroke, Kidney failure and heart attack, yet many people do not take in enough of this nutrient.

3. Kale: 1,100% more vitamin K than the recommended daily amount, more iron than beef per calorie, 90 grams more calcium than milk per serving, kale is the power-food that will change your life! In vegan and alkaline circles kale has long been known for its benefits but here's a quick fun fact. Did you know kale is also a brain super-food? The NIH found that omega 3's in kale improve memory, cognitive function and overall performance!

4. Portobello Mushrooms: These are an absolute favorite for your alkaline taste buds as they're fun to cook on the grill and eat like a burger! But get this, Portobello mushrooms are high in conjugated linoleic acid (CLD) which has cancer preventing properties and anti-aging effects! This powerful meat replacement is also high in B-vitamins which boost energy, cognitive function and help to keep cholesterol levels in check!

5. Garbanzo Beans: Better known as chickpeas, you can't have an alkaline food list without including this multi-functional tasty treat! Plus its nutritional resume is off the charts! Chickpeas are rich in plant-based protein making it a go to for those looking to build muscle without eating meat. The protein combined with its high fiber count make for the perfect combination in regulating blood sugar levels. A DOI study showed that people who ate a meal with 200 grams of chickpeas had a 21% decline in their blood sugar, as opposed to

when they ate a similar amount of whole-grain cereal or white bread.

By becoming more mindful of what we consume and adding alkaline fruits and vegetables to our lifestyle, we're not only flushing the mucus and toxins out of our body, we're boosting our overall health and protecting ourselves against the effects of aging, mental decline and numerous diseases. Start loving yourself by loving your cells! As the great Dr. Sebi once stated: "Love should begin with you. Once you love you, you love the whole world. It's delicious."

A bit of history regarding plant based eating, before colonization our African ancestors ate a predominantly plant based diet. Before slave-traders introduced domesticated animals for consumption, African people were gatherers of roots, corns, seeds and edible flowers. It doesn't come as a shock when you consider the abundance of greenery available on the African continent, as opposed to the cold terrain of Europe. Also to be considered is the fact that there was no printed money during those times and all of the natural resources such as gold and diamonds were an African commodity. Therefore; livestock, guns and alcohol were used to barter. Nonetheless, it turns out that the ancestors were quite mindful of what they consumed.

When we speak of being mindful as it pertains to the food we eat, it provides a great opportunity to exercise our mental. Do you know how empowering it is to exercise your WILL over your own emotions and cravings? Something as simple as eating foods that benefit you & choosing not to succumb to the cravings for foods that do not serve you. This is STRENGTH OF THE MIND (and a fun practical way I like to play out the victory of Heru over Set)! The act of mindfully choosing what best serves us with something as simple as food will go a long way in strengthening the mind to consistently make choices that are in our best interest!

On a consistent basis we must strive to never be enslaved by our emotions, ego, cravings and sensations! The WILL must be stronger than those faculties, if not we will certainly be left vulnerable to the WILL of others who will use those sensations against us! There's a book called "The Art of War", in which the author, Sun Tzu states and I quote "All warfare is based on deception" (Sun Tzu, The Art of War, Kindle Edition). Think about that and how it relates to nutrition. This is truly another layer of spiritual warfare hidden in plain sight. When we consider that processed meats have been differentiated as a group 1 carcinogen by the World Health Organization, one must ask; why is it that meats are promoted and advertised as though they are "healthy"? Most times the quick reasoning being that meats are high in protein, but have we considered what happens when our body absorbs too much protein? Or how about the fact that we can get just as much protein eating a plant based diet. Need I mention that proteins are formed out of amino acids which are plentiful in the vegetable kingdom! The "need" for animal protein is merely a marketing ploy, a myth aimed at striking fear into the public, then in turn using that fear to sell products that are actually harmful to us. Now that is some "Magick" for you!

If we look at food from a spiritual science standpoint, we should ask ourselves what happens with the energy of these deceased animals that are consumed? Energy can only be transferred, never destroyed, so despite the loss of outward consciousness in these animals, their true essence remains. It can be viewed then as karma that the animals we kill, in turn destroy us on a cellular level. Yet on the other hand, let's consider the benefits of fruit. This group of food reigns supreme in hydrating our bodies, providing enzymes, and its electrical energy is the highest of all foods. This is significant because energy is what powers the brain. Fruits supply electrical energy to our nervous system which then distributes that energy throughout the body. This makes fruit the most superior brain food we can ingest.

When observing the science of food it all starts with the Sun. The energy of the Sun serves as food for plants through the process of photosynthesis. The plants are then consumed by animals, which humans then consume also for energy. But the fact of the matter is we can cut out the middle man, the animals, and receive our nutrition and energy right from the plants. In fact, there are even people around the world who survive solely from water and sunlight. They are called "Breatharians" and they believe that humans can survive with just the life force, or "Prana". Before judging, consider that fact that incrementing fasting is basically a shortened version of this lifestyle. When we eat our digestive system then requires about 25% of the energy in our bodies. Those who practice incrementing fasting and the breatharian lifestyle understand that by not eating they have more energy that can be placed elsewhere, chiefly the brain. I'm not a breatharian, I enjoy fruits and vegetables too much but when we consider just how distorted our belief systems have been, for instance the "Got Milk" era, I can't argue against those who are breatharian without scientific evidence from an unbiased source.

Applying mindfulness to ones eating regimen is a great way to ensure we are eating to live. Knowing that mindfulness is all about internal focus and having our attention locked into the present moment, when we apply this mental focus to what we put in our body we now begin to transform ourselves on a cellular level! Normally when we eat we have no set intention, we're watching T.V., having conversations or we've drifted so far in thought that there is no concern to what is happening within us. This leads us to over eating without ever noticing it. By becoming mindful of what we are feeling internally as we eat, we're able to take back control of our health and raise our vibrations.

Before even taking that first bite let's consider where the food came from, starting at the grocery store. Are we acquiring items that will provide nutrition to our body or are we mindlessly buying junk? Fruits and vegetables have the greatest return on investment for our overall health, so before we sit down for a meal lets first be mindful of our food purchase so we're getting the most bang for the buck!

We're often on a set routine as far as when we eat. Most of the time our circumstances dictate the when, but we should strive to be conscious of not falling into a robot like routine. Our body may not be ready for more food so we need to listen to when it tells us it's time to eat. Is your stomach rumbling, are you low on energy? These are the body's natural ways of telling us it's now time to eat. If we eat just because it's the time we normally eat, we're bored, lonely, or because our emotions are telling us to eat, that's setting ourselves up for failure! We don't want to eat when there is no need, we want to be mindful of our body and eat when it is time.

Now let's say the time has come, our body has sent those signals to the brain saying we're ready to eat! We're sitting down, the T.V. is off, and we're fully present in the moment ready to eat. Now we don't want to eat fast, we want to take our time, notice each bite. Savor the texture, aroma, and flavor of the food. Become aware of your body and notice when you are becoming full. It takes a while for our mind to get the signals from our stomach so we want to stop eating at that point. If we keep going until our brain feels that we're full then we've actually overeaten, we just haven't received the signals yet.

Here are a few mindful eating takeaways to think about during and before each meal:

1: What am I eating and is this benefiting me?

2: Where did it come from?

3: Listen to the body; is it saying it's time to eat?

4: When eating, our attention is on JUST EATING.

5: Savor the meal, recognize the taste in each bite.

6: Stop eating before feeling stuffed.

Something else to consider when it comes to the food we consume, is how we can benefit the most mentally. There are certain foods that contain great amounts of Omega 3's, antioxidants and B-vitamins which are all rocket fuel for our intellectual abilities. To close this chapter I want to leave you with 5 amazing brain foods because again, ALL is mind, the universe is MENTAL!

1. Walnuts - Walnuts are packed with minerals and antioxidants that increase memory and concentration! Studies find that walnuts also decrease the risk of Alzheimer's disease.

2. Blueberries - Blueberries hold the highest level of antioxidants of any food which protects the brain from toxins and aging effects! Blueberries are also high in vitamin K which protects the brain from excessive amounts of calcium.

3. Avocado – Back again! Not only are Avocados alkaline but they're also a superfood for the brain! Avocados are rich in vitamin K, which improves cognitive learning and memory. They are also high in unsaturated fats that maintain healthy skin, hair, and nails!

4. Sunflower seeds - Sunflower seeds are full of omega 3's which help brain function. They're also rich with amino acids that help boost serotonin levels and alleviate stress.

5. Kale – Also making a second appearance is Kale! Kale is a superfood with a laundry list of

health benefits. It offers tons of magnesium which boosts the brains "ion channels", which are basically the electrical switches that build our memory and learning ability. Kale is a top tier brain superfood!

We've covered alkaline foods, how to eat mindfully, and superfoods for the brain! Our best ability is our availability! If we're fueling our body with the best nutrients possible, doing what is in our control to live a long healthy life, we can potentially add years to our lifespan! That's more time to spend with your loved ones, more time to accomplish all that we set out to, and more time to enjoy this beautiful utopia that is planet Earth! When we take all of that into consideration it becomes apparent that what we put in our body has a far greater return on investment (ROI) than what we wear on our body. Body, mind and spiritual health is wealth. Remember the universal law correspondence, As Within, So Without!

IX. To Conquer A Demon (Shaking Alcoholism)

Two tendencies govern human choice, the search for quantity and the search for quality. Some follow Maat, others their animal instinct.
~Kemetic Axiom

Perhaps the fastest way to lower your vibrations and poison your temple is by consuming alcohol. This Demon lowers our inhibitions, allowing us to be controlled by impulse, emotion and ego. I refer to it as such because in ancient Kemet, Set was the metaphorical representation of our lower selves. The lower self being the cravings, sensations & ego, all of which alcohol amplifies. With these libations serving as henchmen for Set, and Set later recognized in

Christianity as Satan, I appropriately apply the term Demon to alcoholic beverages.

One of the most significant stages in the initiation process of the Kemetic tradition is highlighted herein. You see while most persons believe health to be of the utmost importance they still smoke tobacco, eat junk foods and consume alcohol. Two things we must overcome are first our identifying with the lower self, and second overcoming the psychological stronghold it has on us. I choose to dedicate an entire chapter solely to alcohol as this seems to be the vice of choice for millennials (it certainly has been for me as I continue to fight off this demon regularly) and I find it of the utmost importance to attack this subject for the betterment of the culture.

Hidden in plain sight, the word "alcohol" in itself conceals the dark nature of the substance. The etymology of the word alcohol has early roots in the Arabic word "Al-ghul" which means "head of the demon". Interestingly enough, in the Arabic countries of the world alcohol is rarely consumed, in fact it is illegal to do so in many parts of the Middle East. Alcohol in its earliest use, was for the purpose of extracting the core nature of a thing. Still today we see alcohol used to remove essential oils, fats, and other chemical compounds from plants, including cannabis. Therefore, if we take the earliest use of alcohol, compounded with its early definition, one can see that alcohol consumption may be used to extract the demon head of the individual. As mentioned before, a demon is simply our lower self, our emotions and ego running wildly, which is exactly what happens to a person under the influence of alcohol.

    With a blurred consciousness we not only make poor decisions, we often find ourselves easily manipulated by the will of others. This is why I consider alcohol to be a biological weapon of spiritual warfare. The substance is readily available in every middle to lower class neighborhood across the United States. Made available in drive-thrus, gas stations, convenient stores and even grocery stores in some places. Certainly without question we have access to all the alcohol we could desire at every social venue as it removes the filter most people have, allowing them to "open up" after having a few drinks. Now why is that? Why would a substance that lowers our inhibitions, causes Cancer (Alcohol consumption is classified as a group 1 carcinogen by the World Health Organization), and causes a lapse in judgement and decision making so stark to what the individual would do if sober be so readily available? There are numerous answers to this question of course, but perhaps the better question would be how great of an impact would it have on the African American community if each of us made a conscious effort to refrain from alcohol use? We would have less Kidney and Liver related diseases that have shortened the lives of many, we would have less violent altercations that stemmed from the use of alcohol, and perhaps the greatest of all, we would have more loving households kept together without domestic disputes that arise, or the lapses in judgement leading to infidelity. These are just some of the effects caused by letting our impulse and cravings get the best of us and consuming alcohol.

A fact that should be taken into great consideration for the black community in America as it relates to alcohol is this: Rum and other alcoholic beverages played a crucial part in the Atlantic slave trade. Alcohol was introduced to Africa as a form of currency and European slave traders would provide alcoholic beverages to all those involved in the securing of slaves. Furthermore, we should take notice of how Frederick Douglass described the use of alcohol by slave owners, and ask ourselves has much changed today? Here's a passage from his autobiography of importance to the topic:

"Their object seems to be, to disgust their slaves with freedom, by plunging them into the lowest depths of dissipation. For instance, the slaveholders not only like to see the slave drink of his own accord, but will adopt various plans to make him drunk. One plan is, to make bets on their slaves, as to who can drink the most whisky without getting drunk; and in this way they succeed in getting whole multitudes to drink to excess. Thus, when the slave asks for virtuous freedom, the cunning slaveholder, knowing his ignorance, cheats him with a dose of vicious dissipation, artfully labeled with the name of liberty. The most of us used to drink it down, and the result was just what might be supposed; many of us were led to think that there was little to choose between liberty and slavery. We felt, and very properly too, that we had almost as well be slaves to man as to rum. So, when the holidays ended, we staggered up from the filth of our wallowing, took a long breath, and marched to the field, feeling upon the whole, rather glad to go, from what our master had deceived us into a belief was freedom, back to the arms of slavery." (Frederick Douglass, The Autobiography of Frederick Douglass: Narrative of the Life of Frederick Douglass an American Slave, 1845)

Most people consume alcohol for a relief, relaxation or "to take the load off" (A corny statement in my opinion but you get it). Some because it makes them more sociable when they otherwise may not be comfortable in certain settings. More than who care to admit it, drink daily because after years of consumption their bodies have become attached to the point that they experience physical and psychological distress without alcohol. What sticks out to me is that no matter the reason, all are seeking something external of themselves to provide them with a more desirable state of being. That is the fundamental issue engraved in alcoholism, drug abuse, porn addiction, and the latest vice, social media dependency.

Mindfulness Meditation gives us a leg up in shaking alcoholism. As of the time of this writing, Mindfulness has been shown to be the best treatment for addiction by the National Institute of Health.

Alcoholism, just as any addiction, preys on our impulses. It's the sudden "urge" to indulge that consumes and leads to repeated use. The key to overcoming the behavior is to use our will power to rise above the emotional sensation of the vice. Sure, it's easier said than done, especially if we're observing the task focused on the future or thinking about how hard it may have been in the past, but if we exercise our WILL in the present moment it becomes quite simple. In fact, when we live in the moment and recognize our thoughts for what they are, just thoughts, we can see things with a proper perspective.

Mindfulness meditation works to our advantage as it is literally exercise for the mind, which is much needed in order to lift the burden of addiction. What mindfulness does is it allows us to observe clearly the thoughts passing through our mind in the present moment from an objective viewpoint. Here instead of acting in accordance with our craving, we simply observe the thought and let it pass right by.

Here's a quick mindfulness practice anyone can do when an urge enters your thoughts!

1. You notice you're craving a drink. The first thing to do here is relax! Doesn't matter if you're watching the game, out on a date or at home alone. Whatever the case may be, this is all internal, so it takes no planning!

2. Take a deep inhale. Feel the air passing from your nose to the diaphragm. Pause briefly for a few seconds at the top of the inhale. Feel your heart beating and any other sensations in your body.

3. Exhale slowly, again place attention on what you are feeling as the air leaves your body. Continue to take deep breaths.

4. Each time you realize your thoughts are drifting, come back to your breathing. This is how you return your attention to the present moment. The breath is your anchor to stay present (Mala

beads also work as an anchor during meditation).

5. Repeat to yourself a few affirmations, here are some examples: "I have joy within", "I'm stronger than temptation", or "I have control over my actions".

6. Continue for as long as you like.

What really helped me on my journey was to realize that I never want to live a life acting blindly in accordance to the WILL of others. What I mean is realizing that most of our actions have been scripted for the benefit of a select few, so now I write my own script! Alcohol is marketed in such a way that it appears to give us the vibe of a happy life, so most times people choose alcohol as a source of enjoyment because they may not yet have realized how to tap into that joy and happiness internally! You see, when you know that you are made of same fabric as the universe and that it's a miracle for you to have even been born, real joy comes in living in the breath! By choosing alcohol we are externalizing that happiness, and this applies to other vices as well (chocolate, porn, cigarettes, shopping, you name it). Once we've externalized our joy, we're at mercy to the WILL of others. Whether it's a fancy car, a sports team, even a brand preference! When happiness is externalized to these things, we become pawns to the WILL of those who can provide them for us.

Take back control by living in the moment and having joy within! In that moment of a sudden urge, breathe in that life force energy and love yourself. Then you'll recognize that drinking is nothing more than a low vibrating habit that doesn't serve you. In the time that you would have been drinking you can create a new habit. One that better serves you such as writing a book, learning a new language, or using the money you would have been spending on alcohol through the course of a year and taking a trip to a new country! I hope this inspires you in tapping into the full potential of your infinite being.

I leave this chapter with a poem I wrote on my own struggles in overcoming alcohol.

"We were once inseparable, walking together stride for stride

You made yourself at home inside of me is where you lie

In a twisted sense of belonging, I convinced myself you were to be accepted

With me as it was for the better, but just how lost was I

A force so strong that some nights I was unable to remember

Thinking I was in control but no, your stimulus had me hindered

Definitely should not have been driving, and thankfully I never took a life

Trying to get home moving reckless, like a blur through the lights

You'd seek out and haunt me, standing tall on every corner I'd turn

Speaking to me over the airways, convincing me it's okay to yearn

For your liquid courage as a way to remove every filter from my words

But really your influence causes loved ones, to feel your wrath and burn

Your forces were eating away at me, harshly from the inside out

Leading me down a long slow road headed straight to Gout

So many years of damage, decisions that I can't go back and change

Must rid myself of you forever, before my health switches lanes

You were given to my ancestors, to numb them from the pain of being sold

Brought to Africa around the same time, distilled and given to the young and old

Damn you Amerikkka, every venue and gathering profiting from the presence

Of evil spirits being poured, seeking whoever they may take hold

But how would I do it, what can substitute your liquid medication

Not until I decided to be finished, did I know the power in libations

Then I was awakened to the powers that I possess within

Realizing my own divinity, building with mindful meditation

A few minutes each day, to appreciate existing in the present

Grounded and connected with the earth, balanced by the energy of her essence

Deep breaths in and out, releasing the stresses of modern society

I have illuminated, now ready to give the world my fluorescence

Able to observe the negative thoughts, including the urges that attached me to you

Replacing those thoughts with ones more in line with what is true

Thoughts of embracing the beauty of living and not dulling my life experience

With liquids containing mind altering energies, this was so long overdue

Now clear I hope to reach those who are masked by your false joys and

Engaging in a society where your image, influences little girls and young boys and

Our culture is so inflicted, unable to hear over the frequency of your dark noise and

It's time we vanquish the demon that is, the White Man's Poison"

(Ben Ellis, To Conquer A Demon, 2018)

X. Manifest Abundance!

The key to all problems is the problem of consciousness. ~ Kemetic Axiom

The first step we must take in manifesting abundance is to change our perception of currency and what it means to be rich. The amount of money we have in our bank accounts will never equate to a happy life until we understand that our lives are priceless. It can be easy to lose sight of this mindset with the pressures of modern society, but the truth is that wealth is an inside job and so long as we have abundance within, we can certainly attract the same to us externally. Much like the passage on technology from chapter 7, if nothing else from this chapter I want you to remember this: Money is a servant for human wants and needs, not the other way around. Keep money in its proper place and always remain the master. That said, lets jump right into how we can manifest abundance!

Let's be clear, abundance is your birth right and there is no shame in knowing that! Not to be misconstrued with entitlement, no one owes us anything, however it is certainly a birthright that can be exercised again through application of our own WILL power. We have to move away from limiting beliefs, thoughts like "No one in my family has ever been rich, why should I be any different" or "Money is the root of all evil"! If we internalize that money or prosperity is evil then we will never manifest a prosperous life. Furthermore we must understand that money is an idea and an outward representation of our own consciousness. To grasp this I want you to think back to the chapter on the 7 Hermetic Principles. Everything vibrates, nothing rest, and currency is no exception. In fact, this is why it's referred to as "currency" in the first place! Because it is energy! Now apply the principle on Cause and Effect which can otherwise be referred to as the law of "Sowing and Reaping", and things really begin to get interesting.

Our lives as they are presently, are the effect of countless prior causes. Our future will be the effect of those causes compounded with causes, choices and actions we take presently. This is the same with our financial status as well. Money is the reward for services rendered. Money being the effect and service being the cause. Basic right? Now let's work backwards here for a minute. I personally like to think of my goal then outline my path to get there. What is your dream? What is abundance for you? Is it a dollar amount? A certain type of house? For me, I view abundance first as my eternal connection with all of creation and the source of creation. Then I see that it should be manifested in the physical as me and my family being able to live a comfortable life whether we are working or not. In old time's, natural resources such as gold or cattle were a means of trading and acquiring the lifestyle one wanted to live. Present day, we use printed money to account for the same. That said, don't be ashamed to view abundance for you as attaining a certain dollar amount, I certainly have one. Once you have decided what abundance is for you or what that dollar amount is, I want you to write it down and internalize it (this process is what's referred to as "scripting" in some circles). It should take you some time to come up with this answer if you truly consider all of the varying expenses and factors. Now understand that the goal, that amount or whatever you determined to be your view of abundance, is an effect and a reward. We attain money, land, and all material wealth through the exchange of goods or services, now ask yourself what goods, services or combination of both can I provide that will allow me to attain the reward I wrote down?

    If we are to take our understanding of the divine laws and apply them to the concept of currency, we might arrive at a very thought worthy conclusion. In the Christian religion, a "sin" is viewed as violation of divine law. Christians view divine law as being some moral rule imposed by an authoritarian figure, but that is not in fact the divine law governing all. It is a man-made concept used to keep the minds of the masses in a box. But knowing divine law to be the natural forces governing the universe (vibration, correspondence, polarity, etc.) would it not then be a sin to work against the law of vibration and that of cause and effect? If we are stagnant, not moving forward and being swept away in the never ending events of cause and effect, we are acting in conflict of the natural laws of the universe. Thus it may be said that it is sinful to remain stagnant and not sow seeds in our attainment of the abundant life that is our birthright! For example, if one were to stop going to work or stop working to master their craft and they lose their job or their business fails, it is because they have not made the proper efforts in their own consciousness to use the law of cause and effect in attaining abundance. Yet on the other hand, if one receives a promotion from their job it is not by pure chance. The individual received a promotion due to a cause that they have aligned themselves for. That cause may be merit, it may be that someone retired, or conversely it might be that their boss held a liking for them and he or she exploited the opportunity. Nonetheless it is a cause. There is a lesson to be learned here in that the unseen forces do not necessarily reward moral correctness. It's the reason why some of the most evil human beings to have ever walked the earth were able to accumulate vast amounts of power and wealth. The harvest you reap is a direct result of the seed you sow. I encourage you to sow seeds of good that will benefit all of humanity and the planet. Now let's dive a little deeper into the concept of money.

The fundamental idea of capital has been around since the beginning of life itself. Currency is all about exchange, give and take, and if we look with a close eye we find that our entire planet is conducting business transactions daily! Animals breathe oxygen and exhale carbon dioxide. Plants then receive that carbon dioxide and release oxygen back into the air ready for the animals to breathe in once more. Just like we humans have created the stock exchange, nature has its own Business of Exchange. Our universe is constantly in the business of giving and receiving. The Sun gives energy to plants, who in turn give energy to the animal kingdom. The animal kingdom returns the favor by giving its waste back to the land, fertilizing it for more life to grow.

Just as Nature's Business of Exchange allows for all of creation to live in infinite abundance, by giving and using the example set forth we create our own reality of infinite abundance. By now you may have noticed that the constant theme here is giving. We have to give, in order to receive. A broke mindset is one that takes handouts without reciprocating that energy. This is why folks who win the lottery are more likely to lose everything as opposed to a child running a lemonade stand. The child in this scenario is building an abundance consciousness in that they are learning that they must provide something of value and be of service to receive abundance in exchange. The person who won the lotto, unless they create a plan to put that money to work for them, through the course of time they will see it all dwindle. Therefore to attract money, to utilize "money magick", we have to put something out there for the universe.

In ancient times leading all the way up to just a few hundred years ago, Bartering systems were the global economy. In a Bartering system goods and services are exchanged for one another. Money is simply a third-party inserted into the Barter system. In old times if you wanted fresh vegetables you had to provide something of equivalent value in exchange, maybe plumbing services, clothing, etc. Today we see vocational skills and trades being removed from the grade level school system, potentially a cause to a catastrophic effect. What will happen if the economy collapses? A great majority of people will struggle to survive because they have no way of providing any service to the world around them. While this is a stark reality, it is also true that our generation has at its finger tips almost countless ways of earning money. If you study wealthy people, which you should if you desire abundance, you will always see that they have multiple streams of income. Now more than ever, anyone with an abundance consciousness can set up multiple streams of income and begin manifesting their dreams. Ecommerce, affiliate marketing, investing in crowdfund vehicles, writing eBooks or starting a YouTube channel, the opportunities seem endless!

    A major key to manifesting more income is creativity (using that right hemisphere of the brain, the divine feminine). Identify a need in the world and create a solution. Not everyone who is wealthy has sold their soul, or inherited generational wealth. No, in fact there are millennial millionaires emerging left and right because they are willing to create something worthwhile or they are supplying a solution to needs in the world. Let's take Apoorva Mehta for example. You may have heard of him, his company Instacart saves users a trip to the market by having their groceries delivered right to their door step. This is a prime example of someone identifying a need in the world, creating a solution and giving it to the masses.

By giving, Apoorva has set up himself and family for life. There are countless examples of millennial entrepreneurs giving their energy to the universe, and in turn the universe has compensated their efforts.

Our time is one of our most valuable assets. I mentioned before that time is an illusion and to live in the present, yes I know. But if you want to manifest more abundance you have to get into the game of life, you can't sit on the bench! No one has ever changed the world by working a 9 to 5! I'm not against it, jobs provide stability and a means to take care of your family. Just don't expect to attain financial freedom by depending solely on a job. We just mentioned that the creators, those who answer needs in society are those who are compensated handsomely, therefore by working a job you are giving your energy to the ones who are actually creating. Worst yet, your energy could be fueling a company, government, or organization that directly contributes to the downfall of humanity. Choose where your time and energy are invested wisely. Is that job serving you? Could the time spent watching television be used to express your own vision to an audience via YouTube or a podcast? The opportunities are endless when we are mindful of how we use our time which brings up our next point, PLANNING!

You've heard the saying "failure to plan is planning to fail", I'm sure. Nothing could be further from the truth. Once we have identified the ways in which to go about attaining our goal, we must now draw up a road map. I've setup my own personal road map by starting from the end goal and working my way down into each finite step. Take that number you wrote earlier, or whatever you wrote as your goal for abundance, and begin to dissect the different means to which you plan to get there. For instance, you may have decided you intend to use the knowledge you possess of automobiles to create a blog, YouTube channel, eBook and do some affiliate marketing. Now from that goal you had originally set, you now have 4 potential income streams to help get you there. I would then pour into each of those avenues, one by one, and research how to do each of them successfully. Create a step by step operating guideline for yourself, complete with milestones, a schedule and action items. Divide the 24 hours in the day into parts. If you still have a 9 to 5 and wonder how you will have the time to accomplish all of this, just remember those 24 hours are comprised of 1,440 minutes in a day. Determine how much time you actually need for sleep and eating, time for your family, the time you actually spend "working" while at your job. Many times we find that we have periods of free time at work that can be used to write notes and take valuable action towards our goals. Whether your lunch break is 30 minutes or an hour, I'm sure there is also plenty of opportunity there as well to work on your craft. During your commute listen to podcasts, YouTube channels, or even mainstream news stations that present information on your subject. Strategic organized planning and the execution thereof is by far the number 1 key to manifesting the life you desire.

    The now popular Law of Attraction also carries a heavy load in manifesting not just money but whatever you choose to bring into your life. What most self-help

"Guru's" will tell you is that if you focus your attention and retrain your mind to achieving success, the universe will conspire to make it happen for you. This is true to an extent. You see all truths are merely half-truths in this world of subjective opinions. The Law of Attraction only works if you take considerable action into bringing about your desires. You can fanaticize about owning a small yacht and relaxing there with your family as much as you want, but until you take steps to see what you need to do for a boating license, find out the cost of a boat, financing, insurance information, determine where you will dock the boat and begin taking action on each of these steps, your boat will not manifest out of thin air! The thing about magic is that we are the magic. Until we exercise the "Will" power of our being, the Law of Attraction will remain akin to a Dream Differed. Changing the perception is only the first step, the action phase is where the magic happens! The science behind the Law of Attraction stems from the ancient spiritual science's that gave us the universal Law of Correspondence, which we covered in chapter 5. The law of correspondence in relation to manifesting, reveals that we attract that which we already are within. So if we are to attract more money and a more abundant livelihood we must do as mentioned at the beginning of this chapter and change our mindset and become rich within.

XI. The Spirit of Love

An answer brings no illumination unless the question has matured to give rise to this answer. Therefore learn how to put a question. ~ Kemetic Axiom

The cradle of a civilization, the highest frequency to experience, and the foundation of a stable home is love. Through the years we have witnessed a collapse to this great pillar due to a great many of reasons, but one I want to highlight is the mirage of love. You see society has impressed upon our minds this picture-perfect image of what love looks like and therefore we as a people have placed enormous standards on what we've come to expect from a spouse or in a relationship.
Let's first peel back the onion on what is love, so that we can begin to rebuild the essence that is the Spirit of Love.

In my early journey when my wife and I had just been dating, I identified love as an infatuation with a person. As I matured I thought I knew definitively what love was. I thought it meant to love a person for their flaws, their emotions, their mental make-up which without a doubt meant so much more than the superficial ideal I previously held, yet I still had not fully grasped what it means to truly love another person. But why is that? How had I been able to go all the way until marriage without truly understanding the full meaning of love?

Here in America we seem to have an outside-in approach to love. We gravitate to what is actually the illusion of love, meaning; we follow our initial physical attraction to a person and spend months and years peeling back the onion of a person to find out if we are actually compatible. In tribal civilizations such as the Dagara tribe of West Africa, love has much more of a holistic approach. Love should begin at the spirit level and work its way out. Remember, all is energy so when we recognize that we are all one we are able to love one another just as we love ourselves.

So much of what we see shapes our perception. As previously discussed, imagery is the language of the subconscious mind and our perception gives us our perspective. What has happened is that through film, reality television, songs and celebrity couples we develop this fabricated notion of what true love is and we hold our partners to make-believe standards. This is not to say we should settle, I am against that notion whole-heartedly, however; comparison is the thief of joy and if we fall into the pit of comparing our relationships to what others highlight on social media or what celebrity couples are doing, we'll end up taking for granted what we have been blessed to have in the first place.

So we see the problem. Now let's identify solutions that will expose love's true essence. We cannot love one another without first loving ourselves. You've heard the saying "Hurt people, hurt people", right? Well it's true, and each of us owes it to ourselves to become keenly aware of who and what we are before embarking on a commitment. The lesson from the chapter "Know Thyself", was that we are all spiritual beings having a human experience. We're all one in this field of energy and separation is merely an illusion to the eye. Once we've embraced just how lucky we are to even have incarnated in human form, with the odds stacked against our birth even taking place statistically, it becomes quite evident of the love we should have for ourselves through our flaws and all. From my own experience, the best way to do this was by embracing my own flaws and imperfections and also learning to accept myself fully.

What I had to come to realize was that I am my largest critic. This took some time as I had to apply a bit of mental alchemy and turn what I viewed as a flaw into my own unique superpower. Here's one example of how I flipped a limiting belief and learned to love myself more: I used to sport a short hair-cut and walk around with a clean shave (nothing wrong with that by the way). When I decided I wanted to grow my hair out and wear locs, I became extremely critical of myself because I feared the reaction of others. In pillow talk with my wife I would say things like "I don't want to lose my job", "will this be professional?" and in my own head I'd be thinking "Just play it safe and get a cut". What I didn't realize was that I was placing myself in an imaginative box of fear. But you see fear can be summed up as False Evidence Appearing Real. My job never mentioned anything to the effect that I would be fired because of my hair. In fact, once I learned to embrace my hair as a part of me, an extension to the miracle that I am for even being here alive and breathing, I stopped caring what people think! I wore my hair proudly because I began to love myself more fully.

The same applies beyond just physical appearance. Our inner critic loves to highlight the flaws but we have to move beyond that and into the love frequency. It's an inside job to love yourself more. Despite your inner critic, despite any external conditions pressed upon you, the reality of the matter is that loving yourself begins within. Accepting that there can be no other you and allowing yourself to JUST BE!

To love ourselves we have to stop critiquing and remember to pat ourselves on the back because we each are doing the best we can with our given circumstance. As a collective we should filter comparison because we quickly move to judgement when we compare one another. If I compare your life to that of someone else it can quickly become a situation where I'm elevating one over the other, but it serves no purpose in creating a love filled community. If we are to help each other elevate we have to peel back the veil, use that third eye to see beneath the surface of things and examine the cause, not the effect.

The best part about coming to this realization is that in a relationship we can now love our partner on a much deeper level. We'll begin to see them in a more holistic manner, as a spiritual being also embarking on this human journey. Once at that point we know that in fact, we are actually brought to our significant others through a countless chain of cause and effect, making the union all the more special. Have you ever considered the millions of events that have had to take place throughout the history of the universe just for you to be born? Combine that with the events leading to the birth of your spouse and the two of you actually meeting one another. It's a beautiful thing to sit back and contemplate.

What has helped my wife and I in our union is to realize that marriage has a unique way of taking two otherwise separate lives and combining them in such a way that nothing can affect one without affecting the other. In an almost mystical way, we've created the spirit of our love that lives within the two of us, well the three of us actually as from this spirit came our daughter. I find the birth of a child resulting from love between two people, to be a direct result of that spirit growing so strong that it must incarnate and embark on its own human experience. Despite our separate physical bodies, the spirit of love between the three of us keeps us united eternally.

Now of course my experience with love is one that may differ from that of your own. But the fundamental point that I want to drive home here is that love for self and another all starts within. So many of us have spent valuable time dating a person for ideal external perfections, only to have our hopes crumble because the spiritual journey of who we're dating does not align with our own life purpose. You see in some tribal communities now and going back into ancient times, children were brought up in the village to view one another as brothers and sisters, despite their biological connections. This enabled the young to grow with one another without sexualizing their nature. Once they matured in age, the elders of the village would convene to decide whom they would marry based on traits exhibited by the adolescence. Obviously in our "modern" society today this is completely unheard of and it would be frowned upon to have arranged marriages. Yet and still I believe we can learn from the underlying premise of tribal weddings.

What if instead of searching for a companion by means of appearance and social status, we encouraged our young adults to seek out someone who compliments their own traits and life purpose? For example, an extroverted artistic person might find they are best suited for an introverted methodical person and vice versa. This isn't to say two extroverts or two introverts couldn't complement one another, but in seeking a mate whose purpose in life is compatible with that of our own, it has the potential to bring out much more meaningful relationships that have an underlying connection that can stand to be tested when the infatuations of physical lust and lure are at a low point.

By placing value on what we have to offer internally as opposed to sexualized infatuations, we'll see a dramatic decrease in the divorce rate, lower instances of infidelity, and an overall greater family dynamic. With greater understanding of our oneness with each other and the sum of nature as a whole, I think we will not only foster greater relationships with our significant others, but a greater connection with all of mankind as we are all one.

In closing, we each can contribute to the new golden age if we apply the ancient teachings mentioned throughout this text in conjunction with all the technical and scientific advances of today. It's never too late to become the person you strive to be. It's never too late to love yourself, love your cells, love your partner and love the universe from which we all came and we will return. Our ancestors left the keys, it is up to each of us internally and collectively to open the door and become a Millennial Initiate!

Love and Light!

Ben Ellis

Disclaimer on Quoted Material

Material quoted in this book has been included solely based upon the actual meaning of the words quoted as they relate to the context of the chapter therein. Just because an individual has been quoted in this book it does not mean that the author, Ben Ellis, nor the publisher, CulturallyShifted LLC, condone or support the persons actions, political views or religious affiliation.

About the Author

Above all else, Ben Ellis is a husband and father first! In 2019 he and his wife, Mercedes Newman-Ellis, founded CulturallyShifted, LLC. A family company dedicated to providing products and content for body, mind and spirit. Ellis is a proud alum of North Carolina A&T State University where he studied Media Management. Knowledge that would prove very useful in entrepreneurial endeavors. As a veteran of the United States Air Force Reserves, and having 9 years of experience working in support of the federal government in logistics and contracting, Ellis understands the business of government and applies those principles to the family company.

Born in Southeast Washington, D.C., raised 20 miles away in Clinton, MD, Ellis is very mindful of issues that affect the African American community and is always considering ways each of us can have a positive impact therein.

Glossary of Terms

1. Alchemy: The transmutation of matter or mental states of being. Alchemy is the precursor to modern chemistry.

2. Ausar: Also known as "Osiris", is the Kemetic deity representing the metaphysical nucleus that unites all the separate functions within us as 1. Ausar is depicted as the divine within each of us.

3. Auset: Also known as "Isis", is the Kemetic deity representing the beginning of our reintegrating consciousness to the divine within (Ausar). Auset is depicted as the wife of Ausar and immaculately conceives Heru.

4. Breatharian: Person who consumes all sustenance from air and sunlight.

5. Chakras: Spiritual energy centers in the human body as well as the Earth.

6. Hermetic: Ancient occult philosophy surrounding Kemetic teachings, alchemy and astrology.

7. Heru: Also known as "Horus", is the Kemetic deity representing the WILL faculty of our consciousness. Heru is depicted as the son of

Ausar and Auset, and as the Sun during the winter solstice.

8. Kemet: Original name for the land now called "Egypt", before Greek invasion.

9. Maya: Term used in ancient civilizations of the Indus Valley to refer to the "illusion" of things that are not what they seem.

10. Melanin: Amino acid that absorbs sunlight and creates the pigment found in natural organisms, plants and animals giving color to their outer layer, skin, hair, and eye retina.

11. Occult: Knowledge of the hidden.

12. Pranayama: Simply referred to as "Prana", is the vital air and universal life force absorbed when we breathe.

13. Set: Also known as "Seth", is the evil Kemetic deity representing our lower selves. It is the animal part of our spirit, emotions, ego, and sensations that separate us from the divine within. Depicted as Ausars brother.

14. Tehuti: Also known as "Thoth" or "Hermes Trismegistus", this is the Kemetic deity representing the wisdom faculty of our consciousness. Depicted as the mouthpiece of Ausar, our reasoning that comes from the divine within.

15. Third Eye: Biologically the Pineal Gland which contains retinal cells and is light sensitive, not dissimilar to an eye. This gland is seated in the Ajna Chakra and is depicted in the Kemetic tradition as the eye of Heru.

11 Kemetic Axioms

1. The body is the house of the divine, therefore it is said "Know Thyself".

2. Know Thyself... and thou shalt know the gods.

3. You will free yourself when you learn to be neutral and follow your heart without letting things sway you.

4. Knowledge is consciousness of reality. Reality is the sum of the laws governing nature and the causes from which they flow.

5. True teaching is not an accumulation of knowledge; it is an awakening of consciousness.

6. An answer brings no illumination unless the question has matured to give rise to this answer. Therefore learn how to put a question.

7. Two tendencies govern human choice, the search for quantity and the search for quality. Some follow Maat, others their animal instinct.

8. Know the world in yourself. Never look for yourself in the world, this would be to project your illusion.

9. All cognition comes from within; we are initiated only by ourselves, but the Master gives the keys.

10. The best and shortest road towards knowledge of truth is Nature.

11. The key to all problems is the problem of consciousness.

11 Conscious Resources

Author, Title, Edition (if any), Year Published

1. Dr. Ra Un Nefer Amen, The Metu Neter volume 1: The Great Oracle of Tehuti and The Egyptian System of Spiritual Cultivation, 1990.

2. Translation by M. Doreal (original author said to be Thoth/Tehuti), The Emerald Tablets of Thoth The Atlantean, Revised, 2006.

3. Queen Afua, Sacred Woman: A Guide to Healing the Feminine Body, Mind, and Spirit, paperback edition, 2001.

4. Sobonfu Somi, The Spirit of Intimacy: Ancient Teachings In The Ways Of Relationships, 2000

5. PtahHotep, edited by Asa G. Hilliard III, The Teachings of Ptahhotep: The Oldest Book in the World, paperback edition, 2012.

6. Translation by E.A. Wallis Budge (original author unknown), The Egyptian Book of The Dead, First edition, 1967.

7. Three Initiates, The Kybalion: A Study of The Hermetic Philosophy of Ancient Egypt and Greece. 2012 (intact edition of the 1908 print).

8. George James, Stolen Legacy: Greek Philosophy is Stolen Egyptian Philosophy, 1954.

9. Nur Ankh Amen, The Ankh: African Origin of Electromagnetism, 1997

10. Dr. Ra Un Nefer Amen, The Metu Neter volume 4, The Ausarian Resurrection- The Initiate's, Daily Meditation Guide, 2010.

11. Maulana Karenga, Selections from the Husia: Sacred Wisdom of Ancient Egypt, 2nd Edition, 1989.

www.ingramcontent.com/pod-product-compliance
Lightning Source LLC
Chambersburg PA
CBHW021013090426
42738CB00007B/776